SECOND EDITION

The Articulate Advocate

Persuasive Skills for Lawyers
in Trials, Appeals, Arbitrations, and Motions

Praise for the first edition of *The Articulate Advocate*

"*The Articulate Advocate* shows you how to use your body, brain, and voice to communicate with impact.... It belongs on the bookshelf of every trial lawyer and should be required reading for those learning to be trial lawyers."
 —Thomas A. Mauet, *Milton O. Riepe Professor and Director of Trial Advocacy, James E. Rogers College of Law, University of Arizona, Tucson, AZ*

"*The Articulate Advocate* is a must-read for anyone who must speak well before audiences big or small. For lawyers in court, before the media, or in the boardroom, it is close to malpractice not to read and practice its wisdom."
 — Paul J. Zwier, *Professor of Law, Emory University, Atlanta, GA*

"Following the practical advice in *The Articulate Advocate* is proof positive that we all can get better at what we do. A must-read for anyone who makes a living in a courtroom, [it] belongs on the bookshelf of every trial lawyer, young, old, and in-between."
 — William Jack, *Smith Haughey Rice & Roegge, Grand Rapids, MI*

"A brilliant little book that I highly recommend ... *The Articulate Advocate* teaches you everything you ever wanted to know about oral advocacy, but didn't know how—or whom—to ask. Providing more than a powerful toolkit, Johnson and Hunter convey, in simple language and easily appreciated metaphors, just enough of the science for you to understand how to skillfully use your body's hardwiring and your brain's operating system to maximum advantage."
 — Michael Halberstam, *Junior Fellow at the Center for Law and Economic Studies, Columbia Law School, New York, NY*

"Johnson and Hunter's insights in this book are better than Prozac and Valium for the nervous litigator."
 — Honorable Nancy Vaidik, *State Court of Appeals, Indianapolis, IN*

"[An] indispensable guide to effective courtroom communication. Johnson and Hunter give the trial lawyer an array of strategies ... to overcome public speaking anxiety and to act naturally in a highly stressful and artificial situation."
 — Professor James Carey, *School of Law, Loyola University, Chicago, IL*

"A succinct and clearly written guide that will help every courtroom lawyer get more comfortable thinking on their feet while they speak—and speaking on their feet while they think."
— *Steven D. McCormick, Kirkland & Ellis, Chicago, IL*

"*The Articulate Advocate* is essential reading for anyone who wants to try cases. No matter how many trials you may have under your belt, you'll find many useful and original insights on how to communicate with juries and judges, or simply with other human beings. It is well organized, engaging, and easy to read. I unequivocally and wholeheartedly encourage you to consume it from cover to cover."
— *Carol B. Anderson, Director of Trial Advocacy, Wake Forest University School of Law, Winston-Salem, NC*

"[A] manual such as *The Articulate Advocate* is long overdue. It is highly original, clearly written, and extremely helpful.... I have no doubt that this book will be an invaluable guide to young aspiring advocates and to those more experienced hands who are never afraid to keep learning."
— *Professor Peter Lyons, CPD Training, York, England*

"*The Articulate Advocate* captures all of the helpful tips, insightful analogies, and useful drills that improve your technique in communicating with fact finders. You can't help but be a more persuasive advocate if you take [it] to heart and put it into practice."
— *Frank Rothschild, former Judge and Prosecutor, Kilauea, HI*

"A generation of trial lawyers and teachers of trial advocacy have waited for this book. Here it is: wisdom of thought and instruction for how to speak as a trial lawyer."
— *Thomas H. Singer, Adjunct Professor of Law, University of Notre Dame Law School, South Bend, IN*

"*The Articulate Advocate*, like [Johnson and Hunter's] lectures, represents the quintessential work on presentation skills."
— *Robert Stein, Robert Stein & Associates, Concord, NH*

"The text presents ... a comprehensive treatment of public speaking, from posture and gesture to mind-set and voice. Beginning with how to stand and what to do with your hands, *The Articulate Advocate* goes on to describe the basics of breathing and how to use your voice to best advantage."
— *Russ Herman, Herman, Herman, Katz & Cotlar, review in* Trial Magazine, *November 2009*

"The book is well organized and is equally useful read from start to finish or by consulting certain topics out of order. The experienced trial attorney will find many ideas for polishing an advanced repertoire, and the new practitioner will appreciate the practical advice for navigating the hurdles of the first few trials."
— *Honorable Judith Goeke, Juvenile Magistrate, First Judicial District, Jefferson County, Golden, CO,* The Colorado Lawyer, *September 2009*

"The techniques range from the very basic (such as how to stop saying *um*) to the more sublime (such as how to tap into the jury's use of echoic memory).... The book's no-nonsense approach allows for quick reading and absorption of tips for immediate application in the courtroom."
— *David R. Hughes, Partner, Davis, Pickren & Seydel, Atlanta, GA,* The Georgia Bar Journal, *August 2009*

SECOND EDITION

The Articulate Advocate

Persuasive Skills for Lawyers
in Trials, Appeals, Arbitrations, and Motions

Brian K. Johnson and Marsha Hunter

CROWN KING BOOKS

Copyright © 2009, 2016 by Crown King Books
Published by Crown King Books
a division of Crown King Media, L.L.C.

All rights reserved.
No part of this book may be reproduced, stored in a retrieval system, or transmitted, in any form or by any means, electronic, mechanical, photocopying, microfilming, recording, or otherwise, without written permission from the publisher.
Printed in the United States of America on acid-free paper.
Last digit in print number: 0 9 2 0 1 5 5 4 3 2 5

    Johnson, Brian K., author.
        The articulate advocate : persuasive skills for
    lawyers in trials, appeals, arbitrations, and motions /
    Brian K. Johnson and Marsha Hunter. -- Second edition.
        pages cm
        Includes bibliographical references and index.
        ISBN 978-1-939506-03-0
        ISBN 978-1-939506-04-7
        ISBN 978-1-939506-05-4
        ISBN 978-1-939506-06-1
        ISBN 978-1-939506-07-8

     1. Communication in law. 2. Forensic oratory.
    3. Trial practice--United States. 4. Persuasion
    (Psychology)   I. Hunter, Marsha, author. II. Title.

K2251.J64 2015   347'.075
                      QBI15-600152

Cover and book design and illustrations by Barbara J. Richied

Crown King Books
Santa Fe, New Mexico
crownkingbooks.com

The right word may be effective, but no word was ever as effective as a rightly timed pause.

Mark Twain

Contents

Foreword 1

Preface 5

Introduction 7

CHAPTER ONE
Your Body 11

Understanding Adrenaline 12
Creating Your Own Performance Ritual 14
Controlling Your Lower Body 16
Plant Your Feet 17
Stand Still 18
Flexible Knees 18
Center Your Hips 19
Move with a Purpose 20
Tactical Breathing 23
The Mechanics of Conscious Breathing 24
Breathe In and Speak Out 26
Oxygenate Your Thinking Brain 27
What Do You Do with Your Hands? 28
The Science of Natural Gestures 29
The Art of Natural Gestures 31
Jump-Start Your Own Gestures 32
Get the Feel of It First 33

The Zone of Gesture 33
The Impulse to Gesture 35

The Ready Position 37
The "Invisible" Ready Position 39
Never Say Never 39
The Mechanics of Readiness 40
The Secret Handshake 40

The Three Rs of Natural Gesture 41
Give, Chop, and Show 42
Gesture "On the Shelf" 47
Some Gestures are Distracting 50
Don't Hold a Pen 51

Summing Up Gestures 51

Posture and Alignment 52
Your Neck and Head 52
Align Your Spine 53
Advocating While Sitting 54

Your Face 56
Your Mouth 56
Your Furrowed Brow 58
Eye Contact 58
Eyes and Notes 63

Summary 63

Talk to Yourself 64

Chapter Two
Your Brain 65

Adrenaline and the Time Warp 66
Seeking the Zone of Concentration 69

Echo Memory 71
Thinking On Your Feet 73
Do Not Read. 73
Do Not Recite. 74
Structured Improvisation. 75
Do Not Read and Talk Simultaneously 77
Notes as Your Visual Aid. 77
Plan to Forget 86
Scripting as a Preliminary Step 89
Avoid Thinking Backward. 89
Chunking 90
Structure: Primacy and Recency 90
Attitude is a Tactical Choice 93
Mirror Neurons. 96
Using Electronic Evidence in the Courtroom 97
Summary. 103
Talk to Yourself 104

CHAPTER THREE

Your Voice 105

Listening to Yourself 106
Your Lungs and Diaphragm 107
Intercostal Muscles and Your Rib Cage 108
Project Your Voice with Breath 109
Vocal Fatigue. 110
Your Larynx and Vocal Cords 111
Articulators and Articulation. 112
Warm Up to Be Articulate. 113

Making Persuasive Choices................................. 115
Energy Up, Pace Down................................. 116
Speak in Phrases, Not Whole Sentences.................. 117
The Mechanics of Phrasing............................. 118
Vary the Pace... 120
Use Your First Utterances to Set the Pace............... 121
Begin Sentences Deliberately........................... 122

Eliminate Thinking Noises................................ 123
Mind the Gap... 124

Emphasis and Meaning.................................. 125
Volume, Pitch, and Duration........................... 129

Why Not Just Read?................................... 131
When You Must Read................................. 133

Gestures and Emphasis................................. 134
Monotone.. 135
Conduct Yourself..................................... 136
Be Smooth... 136
Practice Beginnings with Gestures..................... 137
Visualize Your Performance........................... 140

Prosody: The Music of Natural Conversation............ 141
Audible Punctuation.................................. 142
Ending with Confidence............................... 144

Tone of Voice and Attitude............................. 146

Practicing Verbal Skills................................ 146

Summary... 147

Talk to Yourself...................................... 148

Chapter Four
How to Practice 149

To Know vs. Know How 151

Practice: Resistance and Avoidance.................... 153
Practicing with a Mirror 153
Rationalizations That Inhibit Practicing 154
Be Patient 155

How to Practice, Step-by-Step. 156
Run Your Body's Checklist 157
Warm Up Your Voice 157
Speak in Phrases 158
Gesture Immediately................................. 158
Talk First and Write Second 159
Practice Your Beginning 159
Practice Your Ending 160
Practice Transitions and Headlines 160
Practice Jump-Starting Your Gestures 161
When You Must Read Aloud: Practice! 162
When You Recite from Memory 162
Notes and Visual Aids................................ 163
Practice Courtroom Rituals Aloud 164
Make a Video 165

Exercises to Solve Specific Problems.................. 166

Informal Practice Sessions. 173
Practice During Everyday Conversations................. 175
Observe, Adapt, Adopt 175
The Law of Opposites 176

Practicing for the Mental Game 177

Summary.... 179

Talk to Yourself. 180

CHAPTER FIVE
Applying Your Skills at Trial......181

Jury Selection 182
Opening Statement 186
Direct Examination................................... 190
Cross Examination 197
Closing Argument.................................... 199
Summary... 202
Talk to Yourself...................................... 203

Appendices..................................205

Appendix One: Speaker's Checklist 207
Appendix Two: Video Self-Review Checklist 211
Appendix Three: Essential Delivery Skills While Sitting
for Arbitration 215
Appendix Four: Essential Delivery Skills to Argue a
Motion or Appeal 216
Bibliography 219
Index.. 221
About the Authors..................................... 229

Dedicated to our gifted colleagues at learn-by-doing programs at the National Institute for Trial Advocacy, the US Department of Justice, Hillman Advocacy Program, law firms and law schools across the United States and Canada, and from Estonia to Tasmania. You have inspired, informed, and entertained us with your zealous, artistic advocacy. While there are too many people to mention, we fondly acknowledge the late, great matriarch of NITA, head of the DOJ Criminal Division, insightful teacher, and eloquent exemplar of how to talk with your hands, Jo Ann Harris.

Foreword

Great lawyers come in all shapes and sizes, but they share the ability to capture the essence of an idea and express it in ways that convince others of the idea's inherent strength and persuasiveness. The power to persuade is essential, and the development of that skill is critical to anyone who hopes to have a successful and rewarding career as an advocate.

This is hardly a piercing observation; however, speaking as someone who has taught attorneys how to be advocates for over twenty-five years, I can tell you that two things have changed greatly in the world of advocacy education. The first is our understanding of the blend of scientific rigor and individual personality that enables us to persuade others, and the second is our awareness of the need to apply those skills in a variety of settings, only one of which is a jury trial.

Thirty years ago, opportunities for lawyers to try cases in the early years of their careers were far more abundant. I tried a federal jury case—by myself—as a very junior lawyer. While that didn't happen every day, it was not unusual for young lawyers to amass a lot of courtroom experience long before they became partners in a law firm. Now, opportunities for lawyers to get into the courtroom—at any stage of a career—are so few and far between that law firms routinely pay for young associates to take public interest fellowships in order to give them pro bono trial experience not attainable in cases for paying clients. And because fewer cases go to trial, the stakes are usually higher, and clients are more focused on experienced trial lawyers. It is more important than ever for lawyers to be skilled and persuasive advocates, and it is less and less common to have the opportunity to learn that on the job.

The Investment

> *The difference between ordinary and extraordinary is that little extra.*
> —Jimmy Johnson, American football broadcaster and former player, coach, and executive

Few people are born with the ability to effortlessly think and speak publicly, and with fewer opportunities for courtroom experience, it is up to practitioners to get the training we need and up to leaders to ensure that our lawyers have a way to develop their skills. This is necessary to provide the best possible client service, but it is also necessary to retain the best attorneys—the perfectionists who are always looking to improve their skills and obtain any advantage they can on behalf of their clients.

Providing our attorneys with the best training possible is what turns our great associates into partners that uphold our traditions of excellence. In a business where you are only as good as your last case, we can't afford to staff any case with anything less than our best, and we need to raise that bar every time. It is that need for constant excellence and reliable improvement that has led Morgan Lewis to turn to Brian Johnson and Marsha Hunter for more than a decade to work with our lawyers on honing their advocacy skills—whether they are taking a deposition, arguing a motion, trying a case, or even speaking to a group of clients or colleagues.

We are not alone in this. Brian and Marsha support dozens of programs around the country. Among other things, they are responsible for training new Assistant US Attorneys at the Department of Justice National Advocacy Center, and since 1988, they have kicked off the National Trial Skills Session for the nation's premier legal advocacy skills training program, NITA.

Taking a weeklong program with Brian and Marsha is a career-changing event in the lives of their participants. The skills and tools they give you stay with you indefinitely, and I can often tell when someone has had the benefit of their guidance. Not everyone has that luxury, and this book fills the gap for those who want to invest in their skills but don't have access to the in-person or online training program.

The Science Behind the Art

Any fool can know. The point is to understand.
—ALBERT EINSTEIN

Effective advocacy is both an art and a science, and Brian and Marsha have invested decades in breaking down the elements necessary to understand that science behind the art. The book starts out talking about the importance of being authentic. Brian and Marsha know that you can't convince others of anything if they don't believe in your sincerity. Being authentic or natural when speaking to a jury or cross-examining a witness is easier said than done, but it is critical if you are going to persuade the fact finder.

To help you communicate that authenticity—not only to be natural, but also to be recognized as such—Brian and Marsha use science to unlock the art of your personal style. They focus on understanding what is going on with your body when you are publicly speaking and help you control it consciously. *The Articulate Advocate* explains the science of why you talk too fast and why you say "um" fifteen times during your argument. The book then goes a step further to tell you *exactly what to do* to slow down and eliminate those "thinking noises."

Part of my personal style has always been the use of analogies to translate arcane concepts into human values that a jury can rapidly understand, and so it was with great joy that I read the various case studies and analogies that convey practical and helpful tips on applying the skills taught throughout this book. Brian and Marsha's focus on the use of a "performance ritual" to get your body, brain, and voice under control uses the story of a 72-year old retiree, Dr. Tom Amberry, who made 2,750 consecutive free throws on the basketball court without a single miss. How? Dr. Amberry says his mental and physical ritual before each shot gave him control and consistency. Brian and Marsha explain that a consistent "pre-game" ritual can give you the same success in the courtroom, and they help us create and refine our own physical rituals. When they are done, the way that you position your body or gesture with your hands will be second nature, increasing your focus on what you want to say and how you want to say it.

Real-life examples and practical, detailed solutions like these enable you to solve specific problems, while still allowing room to customize those solutions to suit your personal style, whether you are a first-year associate just starting out or a twenty-year veteran prosecutor looking for that extra edge.

Practice Makes the Master

> *We are what we repeatedly do. Excellence, then, is not an act, but a habit.*
> —ARISTOTLE

At the end of the day, advocacy is often the art of the practical. People support what they can understand, and their basic concepts of fairness and honesty drive the practice of law. Brian and Marsha understand this, of course, and their book excels at pragmatic advice.

It is a universal truth that practice makes perfect, and *The Articulate Advocate*'s last two chapters give you detailed instructions not just about the skills needed, but also how to practice those skills (think conscious breathing) and apply them in real-life advocacy situations, including exercises to try if you speak too softly, can't stand still, or have bad habits like saying "okay" after answers on direct examination, among others. And the book is structured with the pragmatism that comes from training thousands of busy, type A professionals, with summaries at the end of each chapter and appendices that serve as helpful refreshers you can refer to time and time again.

This book is an essential part of the tool kit for anyone who really wants to be a skilled advocate. It is an investment in you, your career, and your clients. If you cannot attend training with Brian and Marsha in person, this book is the next best thing. And if you are one of the lucky among us who has benefited from that training, the book serves as a great refresher!

Jami Wintz McKeon
Chair, Morgan Lewis

Preface

Lawyers are required to advocate persuasively in varied settings using different styles of delivery. A trial lawyer may passionately exhort a group of citizens during a jury trial. In that same courtroom, the advocate may adopt a wholly different energy and tone when arguing a motion in limine to the judge, and then resort to yet a different energy and volume when arguing quietly at sidebar during the trial. Delivery changes to fit the circumstance.

A bench trial is something different. Drop the theatrics, counsel. The judge doesn't want or need the histrionics required to persuade juries, so the advocate adapts to that reality.

Motion practice is different still. It demands a unique style, constantly shifting back and forth between a prepared presentation and an improvised conversation with the bench, or not, depending on the judge. If it's a rocket docket, speed and efficiency are of the essence, and the lawyer deals with it.

Different yet again is an appellate lawyer's argument before an appeals court judge, or perhaps a panel of judges when the discussion expands to include several participants. The approach varies depending on whether a given bench is hot or cold, asking frequent questions, or allowing the prepared presentation to flow without interruption. There may be time limits or not. The advocate adjusts.

Advocacy during arbitration is altogether different from the above, as the setting shifts to a conference room, participants remain seated, and procedural rules are significantly relaxed. Another adjustment is required.

The authors of this book understand how different these many challenges are. We wanted this book to assist as many advocates as possible. The first edition focused on courtroom communication skills for trial lawyers. We have expanded this second edition to make it inclusive of jury trials, bench trials, mock trials, motion practice, appeals, and arbitrations.

Broadening the scope of this book presented us with a particular challenge when describing the different people listening to the advocate. We chose not to list them repeatedly, opting instead for the singularly inclusive word "listener" or "listeners." We trust the reader to understand our intention and to implicitly apply any given technique to the forum and listeners most appropriate to your situation.

In addition, after more than three decades of working exclusively with lawyers, we are familiar with the enthusiastically contrarian instincts of many attorneys. It is part of the job to look for the weaknesses in any given idea, revealed in comments such as "You wouldn't do that *all* the time!" or "That technique won't work in *every* setting!" Objection sustained, counsel. Please understand that we do not mean to suggest that every one of our techniques applies to every advocate in every forum every time. Shakespeare had the perfect solution when he wrote, "Let your own discretion be your tutor." We agree. When it comes to advocacy, one size does not fit all and does not fit all the time.

One of the sensitivities every communicator needs to refine is the ability to adapt to a specific situation. Make the choice that works for you in the setting in which you work. Your goal is to be the articulate advocate—always, in all ways.

Introduction

This book will give you the tools to develop, explore, and expand a distinctly individual style adaptable to any advocacy challenge. That style has to be personal and authentic. You cannot simply mimic a mentor or copy what works for your colleagues, although you may find inspiration in these role models. Your style is a unique combination of elements involved in the control and coordination of your body, your brain, and your voice. To discover—or to polish, if you are well along in your career—your identity as an articulate advocate, you should experiment with the varied stylistic elements described in this book, and find those that suit you. Because no single choice works all the time, or under all circumstances, your style ultimately will consist of many diverse elements reconfigured and adapted to meet any challenge you confront.

Persuasive style is not based on pretending, acting, or faking it; you must look, sound, and feel authentic to be believable. It may seem logical simply to tell yourself to "be natural" or "be yourself," but that is only part of the solution—for the challenge of being natural is complicated by a surprising paradox.

The Paradox of Naturalness

The word "natural" has many definitions: here it refers to the way you speak, think, and behave regularly and consistently in the course of daily life. If you do something often, it's natural; if you don't, it's not. Some of these *natural* behaviors will make you look and feel *unnatural* when public speaking. And as an advocate you need to consciously employ certain *unnatural* behaviors to look and feel *natural*. Thus, the paradox! To complicate the issue, most people remain unaware of their natural behaviors due to this polarity in human behavior: When you are *natural*, you are not *self-conscious*. When you are *self-conscious*, you don't feel *natural*. Therefore, you can't just tell yourself to "be natural," because it is unlikely you are fully *conscious* of what your *natural* behavior is. What you need is technique.

Your Body

Consider some of the physical behaviors you display while engaged in everyday conversation. As you speak with a colleague, you unconsciously exhibit certain mannerisms. Perhaps you push your eyeglasses up on your nose, or brush your hair from your face. You may jingle the change in your pocket, fiddle with a pen, or shift your weight back and forth from one leg to the other. Neither you nor your colleague is likely to be aware of, or distracted by, these behaviors. They are normal, unconscious, and natural.

Now imagine that you're standing up in court to address a judge or jury, or sitting while talking to an arbitrator. You tell yourself to be natural, and your body follows that instruction exactly. You shift your weight back and forth, push your glasses up on your nose, brush your hair from your brow, fiddle with your pen, and jingle the change in your pocket. Do these behaviors make you look "natural" to the listener? No, far from it.

The paradox of naturalness emerges and causes your perfectly normal behaviors to look unnatural. When energizing adrenaline is added to the experience, your body unconsciously engages in these natural actions with extra vigor. More frequent rocking, shifting, pushing, brushing, fidgeting, and jingling make you look increasingly uncomfortable and unnatural. While advocating—when a certain level of formality and self-control is expected—the natural mannerisms that go unnoticed in conversation appear conspicuous and unnatural. What a paradox! Clearly, "being natural" is not the best method for discovering your personal style.

Your Brain

Another example of this paradox relates to your thought process. How often do you turn to someone you know well and ask questions to which you already know the answers? When was the last time you asked a good friend or colleague an extended series of questions beginning with "What's your name? Where do you live? Are you married?" If you asked such questions, your friend would think you were suffering from temporary amnesia. Because you already know the answers, such questions seem decidedly odd.

Yet those are precisely the questions you ask your witnesses during direct examination. You ask questions to which you know the answers—indeed, *only* questions to which you know the answers. Your questions must be worded correctly, asked with appropriate curiosity, and sound spontaneous. Your examination should be as effortless as a natural conversation, not scripted and rehearsed.

Your Voice

You must be able to speak loudly enough for your voice to fill the room. If you are a soft-spoken person by nature, this may feel completely unnatural to you. Yet, should the judge bark, "Counsel, speak up. We can't hear you!" you can't respond, "Sorry, your honor, that wouldn't be natural for me." Authoritative audibility is required in advocacy, whether it is natural for you or not. Further, you must be able to control the pace at which you speak; rid your speech of "thinking noises"; assess how emphatic your most persuasive arguments are; and choose the right word when the pressure is on. The ability to make conscious decisions about using your voice and speaking with finesse is a job requirement for advocates.

Technique

Clearly, just "being yourself" won't make you a persuasive advocate, nor will instructing yourself to "be natural." To discover your authentic, personal style, you need a solid technique that will provide you with reliable answers to all those challenging questions about how to look, sound, and feel natural. How you control your body influences your ability to use your brain to think clearly and your voice to speak persuasively. As you develop and refine this technique, you will pass through self-consciousness to self-awareness and, finally, to self-control. Once you have mastered a technique, the skills of advocacy become second nature.

Chapter One
Your Body

For advocates, the name of the game is to look confident, comfortable, and credible. The way you stand, move, breathe, gesture, and focus your gaze significantly affects how a listener perceives you. As judges, jurors, or arbitrators listen to what you say, they unconsciously scrutinize your physical behavior and assess your credibility. If your demeanor signals nervousness and discomfort, you will be less convincing. But if you act confident and enthusiastic in your role as zealous advocate, you will be persuasive. To achieve this initial goal—looking dynamically at ease and believable at all times, even when feeling nervous—requires a fail-safe technique for controlling your body.

Understanding the function of adrenaline is of paramount importance to this process; few things have greater impact on an attorney's performance. Feelings of anxiety and excitement inevitably trigger the flow of adrenaline, which sends excess energy coursing through your system. This leads many advocates to pace or sway, take fast and shallow breaths, gesture awkwardly, and fidget with their hands. Even the eyes are affected by adrenaline: nervous energy makes it hard for the eyes to focus, and they tend to flit around the room, depriving the listener of eye contact and the advocate of concentration.

By learning to control your breath, as well as the movement of your legs, arms, hands, and eyes, you can channel the power of adrenaline and dictate how your body responds to it.

With guided practice, you will discover how to instruct your body to act in an appropriate and effective way. You can gain conscious control of your body by making desired behaviors part of a performance ritual. You will look comfortable and confident from the very beginning of every presentation, regardless of how you may feel.

Understanding Adrenaline

Adrenaline is a natural hormone dispensed by the adrenal glands. It flows through your body when your instinct signals a need for extra energy, perhaps to defend yourself, run away, or respond to the pressure of performance.

Performance pressures often take a positive form, such as excitement or anticipation. When athletes talk of "being pumped" for the big game, they are responding to that adrenaline being pumped, literally, by their bodies in anticipation of performance. Adrenaline also assists athletes by producing the extra energy needed to throw a ball farther or run faster, and by helping them to concentrate and focus the mind in the heat of competition. Likewise, adrenaline can be a positive factor for the advocate.

The body also releases adrenaline in response to negative pressures, such as nervousness, anxiety, and panic. Excess nervous energy often is referred to as the fight-or-flight syndrome, because adrenaline energizes and animates muscles in our arms to help us fight and in our legs to help us flee.

Although our need to outrun predators has been reduced in modern society, thankfully, we're all familiar with adrenaline-induced energy; it makes your limbs tremble. If you stand up to speak and feel your hands shaking, this is the result of adrenaline preparing your arm muscles to fight. If you feel your knees knocking, adrenaline is pumping extra energy into your thighs and quadriceps to prepare you to run from a threat. The trembling occurs because every muscle in your body is paired with another muscle—for example, biceps and triceps work together to move your forearm—and when adrenaline energizes both simultaneously, they tense and pull against each other, causing your arms or legs to shake.

The common form of nervousness known as "having butterflies in your stomach" takes place in the muscles of respiration. The flutter of those metaphorical butterflies occurs when the diaphragm and intercostal muscles in the ribs pull against each other in response to adrenaline. As you speak, you feel a trembling, which sometimes becomes audible. Your voice shakes or cracks when this excessive muscular tension robs you of adequate breath support, without which you will not be loud enough to be heard. Chances are good you will be so distracted by those butterflies that you won't be your most articulate, persuasive self.

For many advocates, adrenaline pumps because of an ever-shifting balance between excitement and nervousness. It is not only invigorating to confront the challenge of speaking effectively, it is also nerve-wracking—often just a little, sometimes quite a lot. Even seasoned lawyers admit that they experience this phenomenon. Although it is impossible to predict how much adrenaline you will generate at any given moment, it is guaranteed that you will feel the effect of at least *some*. Regardless of the cause of your adrenaline rush, the secret is to channel its corresponding energy in the most effective and appropriate way.

If adrenaline isn't channeled and released, it triggers various inappropriate, unconscious mannerisms that make you look and feel ill at ease. However, if you learn to recognize the impulses to fight, flee, or freeze, you can counter adrenaline's negative effects by proactively gaining control of specific parts of your body.

You may feel an extra rush of adrenaline as you prepare to face your fact finder or witness. Conscious control of your behavior can be established by counting several seconds of silence before you begin to speak. During this silence, run through a short physical checklist in order to prepare your body and focus your mind. Olympic athletes use just such an anticipatory silence to prepare to dive into a pool, ski down a mountain, or race around a track.

Creating Your Own Performance Ritual

In 1992, a 72-year-old retiree walked onto a basketball court in Riverside, California, and made 2,750 consecutive free throws without a miss. Dr. Tom Amberry, who had such confidence in his technique that he brought along ten witnesses who signed affidavits for his submission to the *Guinness Book of World Records*, readily admits he is not a great athlete and never was. So how did he accomplish such a feat? He had a great technique. In his book *Free Throw: 7 Steps to Success at the Free Throw Line,* he describes the mental and physical ritual that gave him such astonishing control and consistency. Every move Dr. Amberry made prior to each shot was part of an unvarying routine. During the silence between shots, he went through a physical checklist. How he planted his feet, how he breathed, how many times he bounced the ball, how his fingers held the ball, how he focused his eyes on the basket—every move was precisely the same 2,750 times. Because his ritual was so consistent, he achieved remarkable results on the basketball court. As demonstrated by Amberry's amazing accomplishment, consistent ritual can help you achieve similar success as an advocate.

Sports psychologists teach that if you want to perform at a high level, you need a consistent mental and physical ritual on which to base your performance. The function of this ritual is to enable the mind, through repetition and practice, to control the body, and to enable the body to control the mind. Together, body and mind help control emotion.

To achieve a consistently effective style, devise and refine a physical ritual for use every time you stand up to speak. In time, this routine will become "second nature"—behavior that looks natural, but is actually the result of technique and diligent practice.

Reliance on a physical ritual frees your brain's prefrontal cortex (the area of your brain responsible for higher intellectual function) from being distracted by pacing, fidgeting or gesturing, and it ensures that your body's actions will be governed by your motor cortex, the brain's overseer of natural automatic functions. Your prefrontal cortex can then focus on more important things, such as what you want to say and how you want to say it. By ritualizing your physical actions, you engage your instinct to move and gesture naturally.

For your own ritual, start with your feet and move up your body to your head. Use a mental checklist to position and align your feet, knees, hips, breath, arms, face, and eyes. Running through this quick checklist will help you get control of your body, positioning and aligning yourself for optimum performance every time you stand to speak.

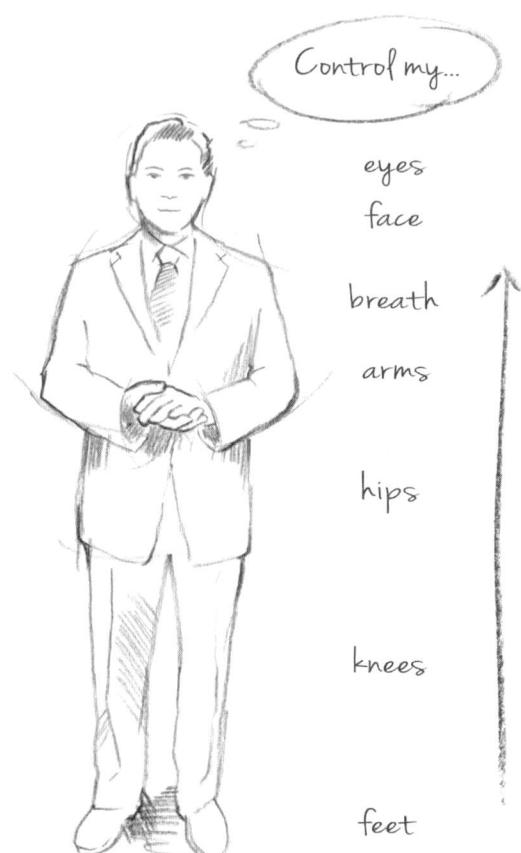

Think from the bottom up, focusing briefly on each part of your body. Use your own body as a mnemonic device to memorize your physical ritual.

Controlling Your Lower Body

In most sports, athletes start by planting their feet in the proper stance. The golfer adopts a stance and then swings a club. The baseball player ritualistically plants both feet in the batter's box and then swings a bat. The basketball player finds a stance on the free throw line and then shoots. As an advocate, begin by planting your feet on the courtroom floor.

Plant Your Feet

Stand with your feet a comfortable distance apart. Don't place your feet so close together that your shoes touch; this stance is too narrow for a solid, comfortable foundation. Do not adopt a stance that is too wide or you will look like a gunslinger in a Western; somewhere between the extremes of too narrow and too wide is a stance that is just right. Avoid standing with your feet in perfect parallel position, as if you are gliding along on skis. Such perfect symmetry can make you look slightly square and wooden, like a soldier at attention. Don't cross your ankles, which looks too casual. Instead, try standing with your feet slightly asymmetrical and out of perfect alignment with each other. Slight asymmetry in the stance makes your body look more relaxed.

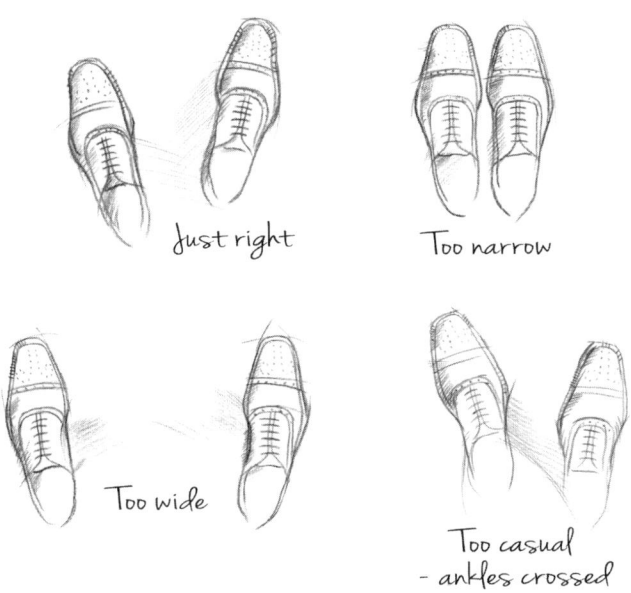

Stand up and experiment right now with finding the right stance for you. Better yet, stand in front of a floor-length mirror so you can see how your stance looks. Once you are satisfied, use it every time you stand up in court. Soon it will become second nature, and your body, just like an athlete's, will do it automatically, without your needing to think about it.

Adopt your stance in the moment before you speak. Do not utter a word until you have planted your feet and are standing still. Then, pause for another moment, take a breath, and feel the floor.

Stand Still

Newton's first law of motion also applies to advocacy: *A body at rest tends to remain at rest; a body in motion tends to remain in motion.* When you plant your feet and stand still, you look calm, comfortable, and in control, and your body will tend to stay at rest. If you start talking while your feet are still moving, your body tends to stay in motion—and may never stop. Random movement will make you appear nervous and ill at ease. Because adrenaline energizes your leg muscles, it is natural—but undesirable—to unconsciously rock, sway, pace, or shuffle your feet. So obey Newton's Law: plant your feet and stand still at the beginning of a presentation.

Flexible Knees

The next step in the ritual is to align and balance your knees and hips over your feet. Your knees should feel flexible. Don't lock your knees by pushing them backward, tightening the thigh muscles and drawing your kneecaps upward. The desirable sensation of flexibility is a feeling of the knee joint floating, perfectly balanced. Think of it as "subway knees," similar to the knee adjustment you make as the door closes and the bus or subway car is about to move. You flex your knees ever so slightly to maintain your balance when you feel forward movement. The adjustment is subtle and virtually invisible. Your knees do not bend as in a crouch, but they adjust enough to flexibly absorb the forward lurch of the train as it pulls out of the station. With flexible knees, your legs will feel comfortable, even when you are standing still for a long time.

Stand up and experiment briefly to find this subtle feeling. Lock your knees backward and feel the sensation you want to avoid. Crouch slightly to move the knees in the opposite direction. Now find the perfect midpoint where the knee joint is floating and flexible. On the checklist, add these flexible knees to your planted feet as you continue to move up your body.

Center Your Hips

Center your hips over your feet and knees. This balances the weight of your torso evenly over both legs, allowing each leg to share the load equally. Although it may temporarily feel comfortable to stand with your body weight and hips shifted off to one side, this off-center position puts most of your body's weight onto a single leg. Eventually that leg gets tired and your body shifts the weight to your other leg. Soon your body is rocking side to side, as each leg in turn tires and shifts the burden to the other. This rocking motion distracts the listener and

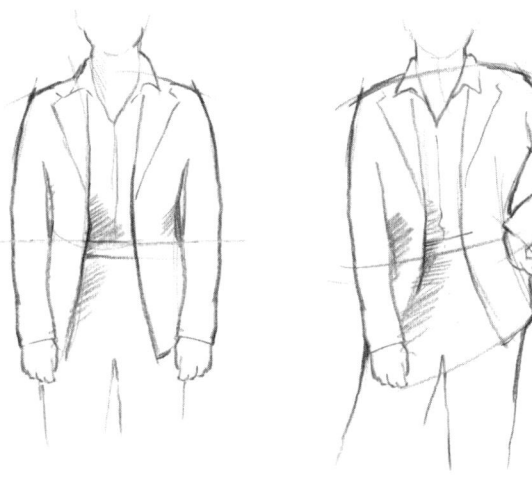

Do this   Not this

makes you look nervous. Note that some looseness and flexibility of your body is desirable, however; you shouldn't feel as if you've been sunk in concrete. So, avoid both repetitive rocking and absolute rigidity.

For women wearing high heels, be aware that they can subtly shift your weight forward onto your toes, causing the buttocks to shift backwards and up. This position shortens and tenses the muscles of your lower back. To counteract this, consciously center your pelvis over your feet and rotate it forward slightly—dancers refer to this as "tucking the tail bone." This will lengthen and relax the muscles in your lower back.

Once you have planted your feet, softened your knees, and centered your hips, you have conscious control of the biggest muscles of your body: buttocks, thighs, and calves. This allows you to control your adrenaline and stand still, even if you are feeling nervous. When you first stand up in court, start by standing still; then, later on, make a conscious decision about when and where to move, assuming the judge allows it. Some judges insist that lawyers remain standing behind a lectern unless they need to approach the witness stand with an exhibit. In some jurisdictions, you must stay at a lectern so a microphone can record the proceedings. If that is what the situation demands, you must be able to comply comfortably. If a judge allows you the freedom to move, do so with a purpose.

Move with a Purpose

Your movement in a courtroom is completely at the discretion of the judge. Some judges require that you ask permission every time: "May I approach the witness, your honor?" Others may give you more general permission to move as you wish. Know what your judge will allow and adjust your behavior accordingly. Assuming you have permission to move, make any movement conscious and purposeful.

A purposeful move is motivated by and connected to your words and ideas. A purposeful move occurs when you walk to a new location as you begin a new topic: "Mr. Gomez, we've talked about your educational background. Now I want to move on and focus on your professional experience." Or, "We've talked about your inventions and patents; now I want to ask you about your licensing agreement with the defendant." Once you have reached the new location, remain there until you are finished and have asked all your questions. This purposeful use of movement assists a jury by helping to clarify the structure of your presentation. The move signals a new beginning and helps to recapture the attention of jurors whose minds have wandered. It invites the distracted listener to re-engage.

Your decision to move must always be made by your thinking brain, not your adrenalized leg muscles. The largest muscles in your body will move of their own accord when they are energized by adrenaline. Powered by instinct and hormones, such movement is truly natural—but it doesn't make you *look* natural, and it certainly isn't desirable. Random movement may feel good because it uses and dissipates the adrenaline in your legs. But resist random movement, and move only when it makes sense.

Movement has power if it starts from stillness, because the change from stasis to motion attracts attention. Incessant pacing robs movement of its impact. Don't be fooled into believing that constant movement keeps listeners interested. And don't be misled by the frequent movement you see in courtroom dramas on television. Actors pretending to be lawyers move frequently because the director knows that movement makes the camera angles more interesting. When the actor moves, the camera pans along with him, giving the shot visual variety. The camera does the work, not the viewers: the television stays in place and the viewers' eyes barely move at all. In an actual courtroom, jurors forced to watch a pacing lawyer have to do the work of the camera, panning back and forth, as if watching a ball in a tennis match. They quickly tire of following a moving target.

Aimless pacing creates visual monotony. The constant back and forth, rhythmic as a hypnotist's watch, can put listeners to sleep. When you pace back and forth, you spend half your time with your back to half of the jury in a courtroom. Every time you turn around and pace in the opposite direction, you turn your back on some of your jurors. They will get bored with looking at your backside rather than your face. It is better to plant your feet and stand still in a central location facing the jury. When you make a purposeful move to a new location, stand still once again. Jurors can see your face and you can look them in the eye and tell them the truth. Sustained eye contact—a key element of persuasive style—is impossible if you pace back and forth.

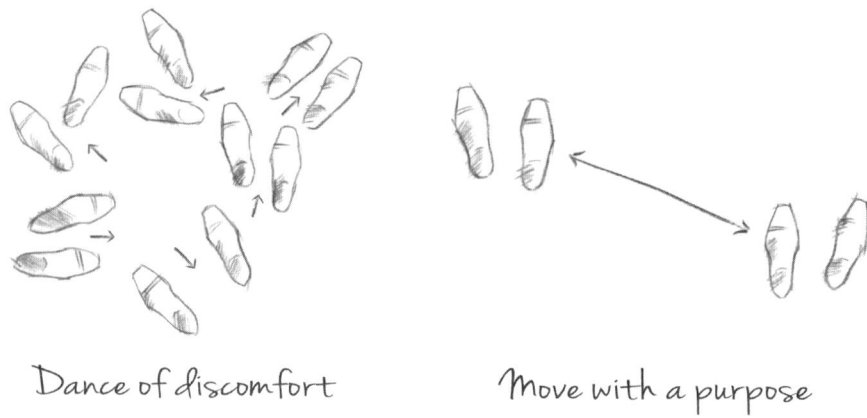

Dance of discomfort   Move with a purpose

How much movement you use is very much a matter of personal style (and the judge's discretion). Some excellent trial lawyers rarely move, while other, equally effective advocates do so frequently. Make logical decisions about when and where you will move. Choose the topic areas—usually the most important ones—where you plan to move, in order to signal a transition into that discussion. You can plan the moves in advance and practice to make sure they work for you. Movement is a stylistic choice, but it is neither a necessity nor a requirement for effective advocacy. If movement doesn't feel right to you, don't bother.

Once you have mastered the ability to plant your feet, float your knees, center your hips, stand still, and move with a purpose, you will have conscious control of your body from your waist down to your feet. You will be in control of your position in the room. The next step is to focus on the middle of your body—the lower torso—where deep breathing occurs.

Tactical Breathing

One of the most useful techniques for an advocate to ritualize is also the simplest: to breathe consciously. The way you breathe is directly related to the way you feel, think, and speak. Once you learn to mindfully control your breathing, it will help you calm down, project your voice, and oxygenate your brain. These three significant benefits flow from controlling how you breathe.

The technique of using breath to control emotions is widely understood. When someone is upset we often say, "You're upset—take a deep breath." Indeed, a few deep breaths have a calming effect because breath and emotion are directly connected. When we are relaxed and at ease, we breathe with longer inhalations and slower exhalations. When we are nervous, anxious, or panic-stricken, adrenaline accelerates our rate of breathing.

Right now, as you read this book, you are breathing unconsciously. If you accelerate the speed of your breathing while reading this sentence, you will begin to feel this connection between breath and emotion. Do it: breathe faster and shallower. The faster you breathe, the more it triggers an emotional response. Now breathe even faster and louder as you continue to read, and begin to simulate the respiratory action of panic. The action begins to provoke the feeling. If you breathe as if you are nervous (fast and shallow), you begin to feel nervous. No wonder—you're beginning to hyperventilate!

Fortunately, the reverse is also true. If you breathe as if you are comfortable and at ease (even when you're not), the action of your conscious breathing can help to control your nervousness. If you take long, deep breaths, as you would while lying on a lawn chair on vacation, you can provoke the feeling of greater comfort. You breathe like you feel, and you feel like you breathe. If you tactically breathe using longer inhalations and exhalations, you imitate the action of your body's respiratory system when you are most comfortable. Take a few full, relaxing, conscious breaths as you continue reading. Feel the difference.

The action of low, deliberate breathing provokes the feeling of greater comfort. While this technique does not make nervousness vanish, it can help take the edge off the anxiety you may feel.

When you are breathing naturally, your respiratory system is controlled by your autonomic nervous system. This is the same system that regulates your beating heart, blinking eyes, and other vital functions. But you can override the autonomic nervous system at any moment and take control of your respiratory system. When you do so, conscious breathing calms you down and you feel better.

The Mechanics of Conscious Breathing

Your lungs are located in your upper torso, protected by your rib cage. The diaphragm, which is the heavy-lifting mechanism of breathing, is a dome-shaped muscle located underneath the lungs and atop the vital organs. When you draw a breath into your lungs, your diaphragm muscle flattens downward toward your waist, creating a partial vacuum that pulls air into your lungs. When the diaphragm moves down, the abdominal wall moves forward and the intercostal muscles pull the rib cage outward slightly. As your lungs fill with air, your internal organs are pushed down and forward as your diaphragm flattens. This is why a deep breath happens in the lower torso, even though your lungs are in your upper torso. It is your abdominal wall or belly that moves forward during deep breathing. When you take a deep breath, you should feel your stomach push forward gently against the belt or waistband of your clothing. This is not a large movement; don't be surprised at how subtle it is. Note also that your shoulders do not rise as your lungs expand. Only heavy exertion causes the upper torso and shoulders to heave up and down.

To feel the full power of conscious, deep breathing, try this exercise: Draw a breath down into your lungs. Now empty your lungs and try to blow out every molecule of air as you exhale. Make an effort to completely empty your lungs. Keep blowing out until you feel an almost desperate need to inhale again, and then blow out the last little bit of air. Finally, when your lungs feel completely empty, breathe in. Feel the air rush back into your lungs. That is a truly deep, maximum breath. Try it again: empty your lungs as you exhale and then feel the air rush back in as you inhale. Activate the muscles of respiration that need to work long and hard when you speak in a courtroom. While you won't empty your lungs like this as you speak, it is important to understand that they have a surprising amount of untapped capacity.

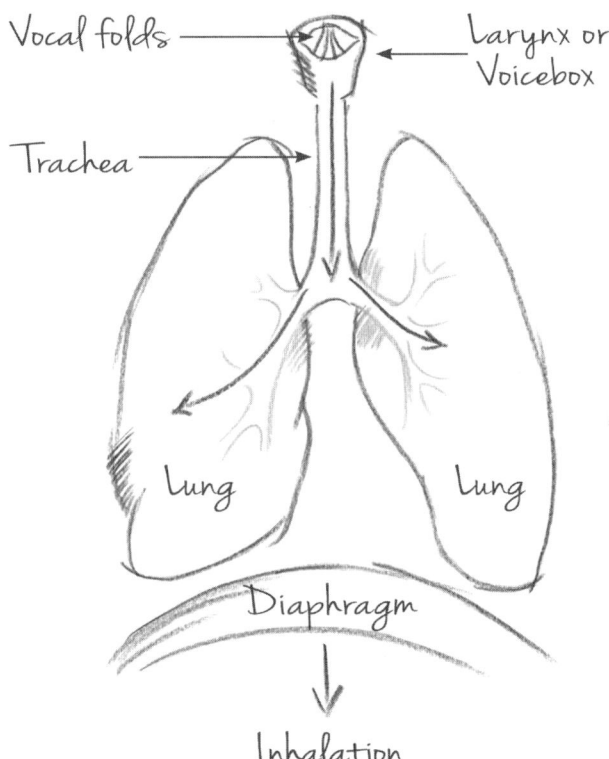

The sooner you get conscious control of your breath, the better you'll feel. Do not wait until you have walked to the well of a courtroom to think about your breathing. Get control far in advance of that moment. A few minutes before you stand up, as you realize opposing counsel is ending her examination, take several conscious, deep breaths. Better still, take those conscious breaths hours earlier. As you walk up the courthouse steps, breathe deeply. As you drive to the courthouse, periodically inhale and exhale slowly, three times. When the alarm goes off in the morning and you feel that first rush of adrenaline as you think of the day's proceedings, take a few deep, deliberate breaths before you get out of bed.

Conscious breathing is also an excellent way to short-circuit the fretting about the future that plagues many advocates far in advance of performing. If you find yourself spiraling down into an anxiety attack, stop yourself with this instruction: *Breathe tactically right now.* Conscious breathing in the present moment distracts you from thinking about the future, over which you have no control.

If you sing in a choir or play a wind instrument, you may have used a similar technique to achieve deep, conscious breathing, which is also known as abdominal or belly breathing. Practitioners of yoga and martial arts use conscious or mindful breathing deep in the torso; athletes learn to exploit deep breathing as part of the ritual of preparing for competition. Likewise, tactical breathing will improve your performance.

Breathe In and Speak Out

Once you are deliberately breathing to feel better, use that same breathing to achieve your second goal—speaking better. Chapter Three will describe the connection between breathing and speaking more completely, but it is important to mention the subject here as part of the physical ritual of preparation.

Stage actors refer to the connection between breathing and speaking on the stage as "breath support." The amount of air in your lungs is what supports and projects your voice. Your voice is loud in direct proportion to the volume of air in your lungs. Less air means less sound; more air means more sound. If you take conscious control of your breath prior to speaking, you then have more air available when you open your mouth to speak. If you are naturally soft-spoken, there is only one way to turn up the volume: use more air. Since you need more air flowing out of your lungs to speak louder, you obviously must bring more air into your lungs as you inhale. That air is then available to put more power behind your voice. You speak on the exhalation of breath from the lungs.

Patsy Rodenburg, a preeminent voice coach in London, described the mechanics of speaking as "breathe in, speak out." Breathe in to fill your lungs, then speak as the air flows back out. The breath flows up through your trachea and voice box, where your vocal cords vibrate by the force of passing air. Start speaking when your lungs are full of air. Don't make the mistake of trying to speak after you have exhaled. Breathe in, and speak out once you have filled your lungs with air.

Oxygenate Your Thinking Brain

You will discover a third benefit of conscious breathing. The more efficiently you breathe, the more you increase the amount of oxygen in your lungs, which then passes into your bloodstream and circulates throughout your body—including to your brain. Your brain needs about 20 percent of the oxygen your body takes in. The more efficiently and deeply you breathe, the more ample the supply of oxygen to your lungs, your bloodstream, and, ultimately, your brain. Your breath helps you to think quickly and clearly.

Since breathing will help you feel better, speak better, and think better, the sooner you begin the process of deliberate breathing and the more consistently you do it, the more control you will have. Just as planting your feet and standing still controls the adrenaline in your legs, controlling your breath prevents adrenaline from accelerating your respiration. The next challenge is to channel and release adrenaline's considerable energy, allowing it to flow appropriately out of your body; for that you need to use your arms, hands, and shoulders.

What Do You Do with Your Hands?

Many advocates struggle with this question. Since you want to look and feel natural, it may seem logical to tell yourself to simply gesture naturally. That is not so easy because you are largely unaware of your natural gestures. "Gesture naturally" is at best a partial answer.

A common yet mistaken answer to this question of what to do with your hands is "Don't gesture." Some people cling to an old-fashioned belief that gestures are inappropriate for advocates. Law students and attorneys are commonly told to place their hands on the lectern or at their sides because gestures distract the listener. There are three problems with this belief: (1) there is no scientific evidence to back it up; (2) it is completely unnatural to inhibit your gestures; and (3) it is not the way effective lawyers behave. If your goal is to be natural in court, then standing with your arms dangling at your sides or gripping the lectern could not be a worse answer.

The assertion that gestures are distracting is an excellent example of unreliable hearsay. Neuroscientists and social scientists who study gestures have discovered that gesture and language are inextricably intertwined in the human brain. Research in the areas of neurology and cognition proves beyond a reasonable doubt that gesturing is an integral component of speaking and thinking. You must gesture in order to look, feel, speak, and think naturally. Gestures not only enhance the meaning of language, they allow the body to channel and release the energy of adrenaline.

Everyone gestures. Some people do it more and others less, but everyone gestures in conversation, especially when speaking persuasively. Reading this, you may be saying to yourself, "But I don't gesture! I know I don't gesture." You may not be aware of it—yet—because your gestures are not controlled by the conscious intellect. They are controlled by instinct.

To better understand this principle, begin to observe and analyze how people talk to one another. Start paying attention to your own gestures. What do you do with your hands during conversations with friends, family, and colleagues? Notice how often your hands move while you speak. How large are those movements? How long do the patterns of gesture last? Watch others, too. As you become increasingly aware of gestures, you will discover an amazing amount of communication—literally right under your nose—that you may never have noticed before.

The Science of Natural Gestures

After a trip to Italy, psychologist Dr. Jana Iverson was inspired to study the origin of gesturing. Her research posed the following questions: Do we learn to gesture by watching others do it? In other words, are gestures nurtured by observation and imitation when children are learning to speak? Or is it hardwired in the human brain—is it nature rather than nurture that makes us gesture? Her research studied children who were blind from birth, observing them in conversation with others.

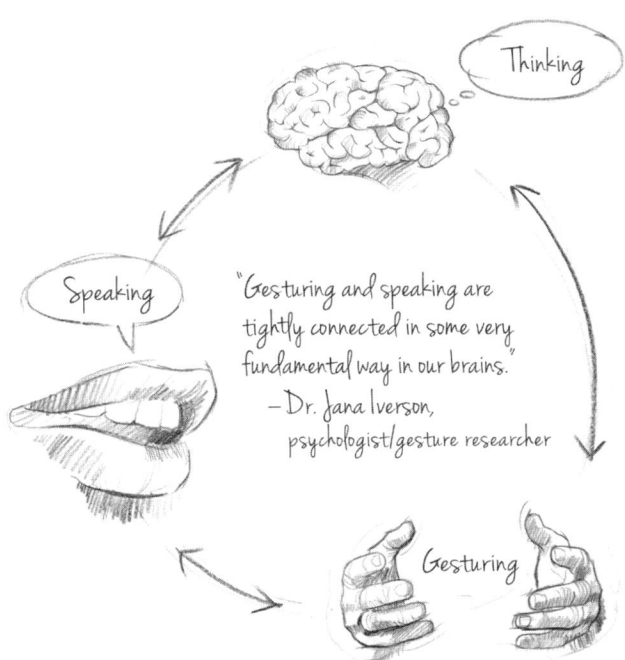

"Gesturing and speaking are tightly connected in some very fundamental way in our brains."
— Dr. Jana Iverson, psychologist/gesture researcher

Dr. Iverson discovered something surprising. Congenitally blind children use gestures when they talk, even when speaking to others whom they know to be blind. These children gestured the same as her sighted control group. How can someone gesture who has never seen a gesture? Dr. Iverson's study reveals the innate connection in the brain between the flow of gestures and the flow of language. Dr. Iverson writes, "The fact that someone who had never seen gestures before would gesture, even to a partner who they know can't see, suggests that gesturing and speaking are tightly connected in some very fundamental way in our brains." Not only do gestures help speakers generate language, but the flow of gestures also assists listeners in understanding what is being said.

The journal *Research on Language and Social Interaction* published a special issue called *Gesture and Understanding in Social Interaction*, in which studies revealed the important connections among thinking, speaking, gesturing, and listening. One study reported that people comprehended spoken sentences *twice as well* when gestures accompanied speech as when gestures were absent. In another study, the subjects were told a short story, then given a partial transcript of the story and asked to fill in the missing parts. The researchers concluded: "Those parts of the story accompanied by well-defined gestures were filled in with greater accuracy." In other words, gestures will help your listeners remember what you said.

Another study in this collection found that "people obtain information from gestures accompanying speech that they integrate with the information that is conveyed in the speech." Your gestures can provide listeners with important information. Other studies conclude that "gestures together with speech can provide the recipient with a more complete understanding of the utterance, that gestures sometimes may even provide a component that is crucial for its understanding." Gestures give subtle clues about intent and point of view, crucial components in comprehension, which allow your judge, jury, or arbitrator to better understand what you are saying. All the research points to this conclusion: if you want people to follow, remember, and be persuaded by what you are saying, you must gesture.

Gestures also help you to remember what you intend to say—and to say it better. Researcher Adam Kendon at the University of Pennsylvania asserts that gestures help speakers conjure the proper words from memory. The journal *Psychological Science* has reported a finding by Dr. Susan Goldin-Meadow of the University of Chicago and her colleagues that people who were allowed to gesture while recalling a list of memorized words recalled, on average, 20 percent more than people who were not allowed to gesture. In other words, gesturing assists your word retrieval and memory. If gesturing will improve your ability to recall and remember what you want to say by a full 20 percent, it is obvious that gesturing is an essential element of your persuasive style.

Further scientific evidence of the close linkage between speech, gesture, and comprehension can be found in David McNeill's *Hand and Mind* as well as Dr. Susan Goldin-Meadow's *Hearing Gesture: How Our Hands Help Us Think*. Neurologist Frank R. Wilson's *The Hand: How Its Use Shapes the Brain, Language, and Human Culture* provides an anthropological perspective to the issue. (See our bibliography for references.)

The Art of Natural Gestures

This science of gesture dovetails precisely with the art of gesturing, as described by the greatest playwright in the English language. William Shakespeare, speaking through the title character in *Hamlet*, offers the following practical suggestion. In the speech referred to as Hamlet's Advice to the Players, Shakespeare's instructions are simple: "Suit the action to the word, the word to the action."

His advice confirms Dr. Iverson's observation "that gesturing and speaking are tightly connected in some very fundamental way in our brains." Art and science agree that gestures suit, or fit, the words being spoken, and the words logically fit the actions of our hands. Gesturing is not emotional or theatrical, but logical.

Jump-Start Your Own Gestures

You have a lifetime of experience gesturing while speaking, whether sitting or standing. Instinctively and unconsciously, your body already knows how to gesture, but you need a technique to jump-start them from the beginning of every presentation. Think about your gestures to get them started; stop thinking about them once they get going.

Triggering your natural gestures is analogous to jump-starting a dead car battery. You connect jumper cables from a working battery to the moribund one. When you turn the key in the ignition, the working battery jump-starts the dead one. Once the engine is running, you remove the jumper cables, slam the hood, and drive off, confident that electricity is now flowing.

At the very beginning of a presentation, the instinct to gesture can be as dead as a car battery at twenty below zero, frozen by self-consciousness, anxiety, or the erroneous belief that gestures are distracting. To jump-start your gestures, think of your brain as the energy source. Connect the metaphorical jumper cables of conscious thought to your instinct to gesture and turn the key. Deliberately gesture at the beginning, and suit the action to the word. Make sure your gestural engine is running.

Get the Feel of It First

When learning how to play a guitar, dance the tango, or swing a golf club, you may look and feel a little awkward at first, until you get the feel of it. To learn a new physical skill, you begin by thinking intensely about the action required, a process that takes place in the prefrontal cortex of your brain. When learning to play the guitar, you painstakingly think about each chord: put the index finger here, middle finger there, ring finger there, and the pinkie finger over here. You concentrate on each chord and make mistakes. Your playing feels awkward. But once you begin to get the feel of it, your motor cortex takes over. Muscle memory places your fingers on the guitar strings. You think "C major chord," and your fingers know where to go.

Similarly, conscious gesturing may not feel natural the first time you try it. Don't be surprised. The gestures are natural, but the conscious activity of the brain telling the hands to do them is unnatural. It is technical, and first you need to learn and practice the mechanics. With enough practice, it becomes second nature. Unlike learning a new skill, such as golf or tennis, you are triggering a primal instinct. Gesturing is an essential element of an articulate style. Don't let a little initial awkwardness frustrate you. Practice the skill until you get the feel of it.

Even though you gesture in a unique personal style, there are some general observations that apply to everybody. As you observe your own gestures and those of other speakers, pay specific attention to how large the gestures are, how long they last, and how they connect to words. Note the specific shape of the hands while gesturing, and where the hands rest when they are still. Rather than focus on the faces of speakers, watch their hands.

The Zone of Gesture

Natural gestures have observable and quantifiable characteristics. For example, conversational gestures are surprisingly large. They move or flow through an area in front of the body we call the "zone of gesture."

This zone is a large rectangular space approximately two feet tall by four feet wide. It extends vertically from the waist to the nose. Gestures rarely happen with the hands below the waist or above the shoulders. This zone extends horizontally about two feet out to each side of your body—almost the full reach of your arms. Even when you are sitting down, your gestures regularly fill this zone.

When sitting in a mall, restaurant, or airport, watch the animated conversations taking place around you and note the size of the gestures you see. When sitting in a meeting and listening to others speak, focus on their hands. Watch how people gesture on television and in films. Watch television with the sound turned off to observe gestures. You will be surprised at how large natural gestures really are. As the title of Dr. Susan Goldin-Meadow's book suggests, start *hearing* gestures. Listen to the words people are saying, but watch their hands. Observe the size of the zone of gesture, and see the obvious connection between speech and gesture.

Gestures often involve the whole arm from the shoulder to the hand. This isn't to suggest that all gestures are large and expansive; many are not. But many use the entire limb. Extend your arms so they comfortably fill the zone. When you feel some "air in your armpits," you'll know your gestures are large enough.

By using your whole arm, you avoid a common pitfall of nervous speakers: gesturing with just wrists or forearms. Anxious advocates keep the upper arms tight against the body, as if the elbows have been bolted to the rib cage. This not only shrinks the zone of gesture, it also limits the size of gestures, making them appear and feel unnatural. Smaller gestures look tight and jerky; the zone of gesture is cramped. The body's instinct for self-preservation keeps the hands and forearms in front of vital organs for protection, making gestures tentative and constricted. Such half-gestures merely reveal a speaker's anxiety, doing nothing to clarify the meaning of speech. They don't last long enough to support and reinforce expressive speaking. The action is not suited to the word, as Shakespeare suggests.

In addition to being large and filling the zone, gestures often last a long time. Watch how many seconds a pattern of conversational gesturing stays active and animated, unlike such relatively short-lived actions as a clenched fist, the obscene flip of "the bird," or the circular thumb and index finger indicating "okay." (These iconic and culturally specific gestures differ fundamentally in duration from the flowing patterns of conversational gesturing.) It is not uncommon for people to simultaneously talk and gesture nonstop for many minutes, especially when speaking energetically and persuasively. In fact, speaking energetically and persuasively *requires* gestures that are long, smooth, and loose.

The Impulse to Gesture

When language needs emphasis but emphatic gestures are suppressed (whether by nervousness or the belief that gesturing is inappropriate), the instinct inevitably surfaces in some inappropriate way. It can reveal itself in the twitch of a finger, the flick of a wrist, or a quick flap of a forearm. These are not complete gestures, but impulses or attempts, revealing that the body is instinctively trying to gesture but is prevented from doing so by self-consciousness or nerves. When you observe these impulses carefully, you can see a direct correlation between the impulses and the words. Each impulse is not just a nervous fidget; it shows the connection between speech and gesture in the brain. The hands know instinctively which words are important and need emphasis. The urge to gesture occurs particularly on those key words that clarify meaning.

When gestures are inhibited and reduced to twitching fingers and flapping forearms, listeners hear the result in verbal expression. When your gestures are restrained, your speech tends toward monotone. Ideas are not delivered clearly and emphatically because the gesture needed to accompany the word is absent or underpowered. Both your language and your listeners suffer.

If you have doubts about how strong the impulse to gesture is, consider how often people plunge their hands into their pockets while speaking. Even tucked deep within, the hands don't stay still. They jingle change and continue to fidget. The impulse to gesture doesn't go away—it is merely displaced, at times to the detriment of both message and speaker.

To sum up: when you begin to speak, make your initial gestures loose and smooth. Why do we say "She is so smooth!" to compliment a good speaker? Because it is literally true. Natural gestures are larger and longer than the constrained, short gestures of nervous speakers. They are also smooth instead of jerky, slow instead of fast. Given the interrelationship of gesturing, speaking, and thinking, being physically smooth with your arms and hands will bring smoothness to your verbal delivery and mental flow.

The Ready Position

No one gestures all the time, not even avid gesticulators. Gestural flow alternates between action, when hands are moving, and stillness, when they are not. Your hands need a neutral position of readiness that can be part of your physical ritual checklist. Before you speak, if your hands are in a position where they are poised to gesture, your gestures will flow naturally.

The concept of a ready position comes from watching experienced lawyers and asking the question, "Where do they put their hands when they are *not* gesturing?" The answer: loosely touching at waist height. Hands and forearms are energized and ready to go, not pressed against the abdomen. The position is loose, not tight. A little bit of space separates the forearms from the abdomen.

Consider the logic of this position. In the ready position, the muscles of your upper arm hold a small amount of tension to keep the hands at waist height. Without that muscular tension, the hands drop below the waist to the classic "fig leaf" position, where they are placed modestly in front of the crotch. The fig leaf is the default, unready position of the nervous advocate. While the fig leaf is a perfectly natural resting position if waiting for an elevator or a cash machine, this below-the-waist position leaves the arms and hands under-energized and unready to gesture. The instinct to gesture cannot easily engage when the arms are hanging limply.

Other positions that prevent gestures from flowing are the reverse fig leaf (hands clasped behind the back, or what the military calls "parade rest"), hands resting on the lectern, or leaning on counsel table. The ready position works because it places the hands in the same location where they do most of their work: in front of the body at waist height and poised for action.

Think about where your hands are when you hold and read a book—directly in front of the middle of your body. That is the same general location where your arms and hands are when you eat, write, compute, or use your cell phone. If you want to gesture naturally, keep your hands where they spend the greatest amount of time working.

For most people, the ready position puts the hands right in front of the belly button, with biceps slightly energized and elbows bent at 90 degrees. Here, they are also right at the bottom of the zone of gesture that extends vertically from waist to nose. By placing your hands in this position before you speak and returning to it when you are not gesturing, you will find it easier to trigger your instinct to gesture.

The "Invisible" Ready Position

When lecturing, we routinely say to our audience, "I've now been speaking to you for forty minutes. Raise your hand if you have noticed where I put my hands when I am not gesturing." How many hands go up? Often none at all, sometimes a few. It's a strange thing, but the ready position is invisible to most observers. This is true despite the fact that a speaker's hands in the ready position are precisely at the eye level of the listeners. Why then, is it virtually invisible?

Listeners focus on eyes, not hands. So you can trust that your ready position—hands loosely touching in front of the belly button—will not be consciously seen by the fact finders listening to you. It's invisible. Pay close attention to all sorts of speakers, both live or on television, and you will observe this ready position frequently—the local weatherman, talk show hosts, or the TV news reporter from the war zone. They all use it; you've just never noticed. See now what has been invisible to you before.

Never Say Never

Should you *never* place your hands in your pockets, behind your back, or in the fig leaf position? Never say *never*. All those positions are viable options to be used occasionally. The question is, when? If you briefly place your hands in the fig leaf position, reverse fig leaf, in your pockets or on the lectern, that's okay. But be aware that once your hands retreat to one of these resting positions they will stay there longer than is desirable, because bodies at rest tend to stay at rest. Avoid these resting positions at the beginning of a presentation. However, once you liberate your gestural instinct and get it going, it is perfectly acceptable for the hands to cycle through a wide variety of positions.

Variety is the spice of life and of advocacy technique. Listening to a witness answer a question, the jury's eyes are focused on the witness, not you. Such moments are a perfect opportunity for the hands to adopt one of the alternative positions. Just don't get stuck there too long!

The Mechanics of Readiness

Your hands can touch each other in a number of ways in the ready position. It doesn't matter how, as long as you can keep them still and don't fidget. Wringing the hands—the cliché of nervousness—is the result of adrenaline energizing the hands to rub each other. Use this energy for gesturing instead. The important thing is that your hands remain still, yet ready to release gestures and begin to flow. Do not rest your forearms snugly against your belly for extended periods of time. That is resting, not readiness.

Adopt a ready position so you start gesturing immediately. If you remain in the ready position too long, you will appear to have joined a religious order. Resist your body's impulse to interlace your fingers as if in prayer. You will find it difficult to separate your hands; even a little tension in those interlaced fingers will lock your hands together.

If you are long-waisted or have short arms, have an ample paunch or are pregnant, you may need to adjust your hands and arms higher or lower to suit your body type. Experiment to find a position where your elbows are still at 90 degrees, but your hands are open and ready to gesture.

The Secret Handshake

One particularly useful ready position is the "secret handshake." It is especially helpful for extremely nervous speakers. To experiment with

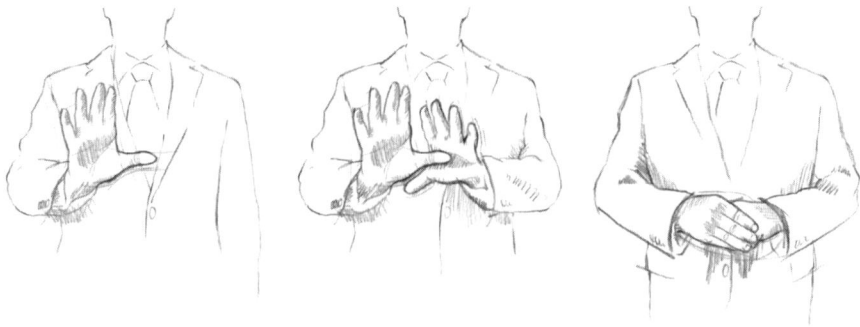

this position, hold your hands with both palms facing forward and extend the thumb of your right hand out to the side. With your left hand, gently grab your right thumb as if it were the handlebar of a bicycle. Pull your hands loosely toward your belly button, and position your hands so that you conceal the fact you are holding onto your thumb. The secret handshake gives you a security blanket—a warm thumb to hold—yet it permits a quick release of that thumb to allow the gestures to flow. It is also far preferable to the common practice of holding a pen.

The Three Rs of Natural Gesture

As you practice gesturing, remind yourself to use the Three Rs: *ready, release,* and *relax*. First, put your hands in the ready position so that they are *ready* to gesture. Assume this ready position before you speak, making it part of your physical ritual of preparation. The second R requires that you *release* your gestures as you begin talking and filling the zone of gesture. Don't wait; gesture immediately. (Specific gestures will be discussed in the next section.) As you speak, your hands and arms will be engaged in either *ready* or *release* most of the time. You *release* your gestures when you ask a question of a witness, then return to the ready position to listen to the answer. Sometimes, for variety and comfort, let your arms *relax*—the third R. Let all the tension out of your arm muscles so the arms drop gently to your sides and hang there briefly.

Once you master the three Rs, you can combine *release* and *relax* to give yourself two additional options. While the right hand is gesturing, the left arm can be relaxed and hanging at your side. As the left hand gestures, the right arm relaxes. In other words, don't always gesture with both hands; the variety of ambidexterity is desirable. These options—right hand, left hand, and both hands—give you five different ways to use your arms while gesturing. Simply cycle through the five positions randomly, using *ready* and *release* most of the time, but occasionally letting one or both arms *relax*. *Relax* is an especially useful position to use when a witness is answering a question on direct examination or a judge is asking you a question during a motion.

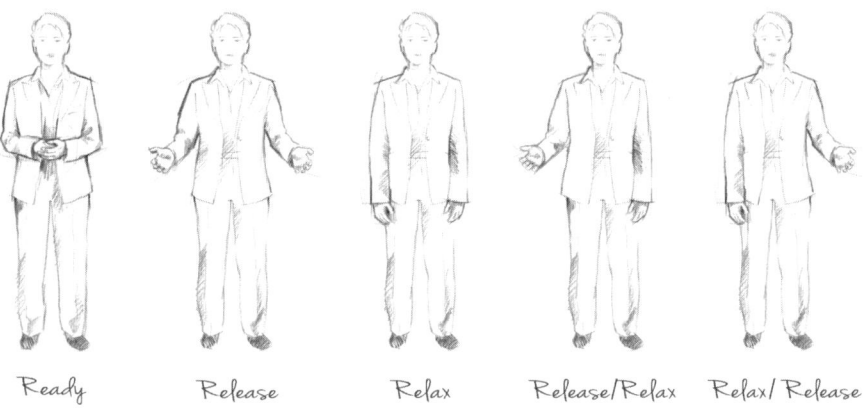

Ready　　　Release　　　Relax　　Release/Relax　　Relax/Release

If you experiment with the ready position and eventually discover that it doesn't work for you, use an alternative. Placing your hands at your sides in the *relax* position can serve as the neutral position when you are not gesturing. This looks fine. Be aware, however, that since the arm muscles are hanging slack, it takes more conscious effort to start the gestures flowing.

Give, Chop, and Show

Once you have placed your hands in the ready position, deliberately instruct your arms to release an initial gesture. There are three types of gestures commonly used in conversation, and three simple words will help you remember your options: *give, chop,* and *show*. Practice them in private until you can use them with confidence.

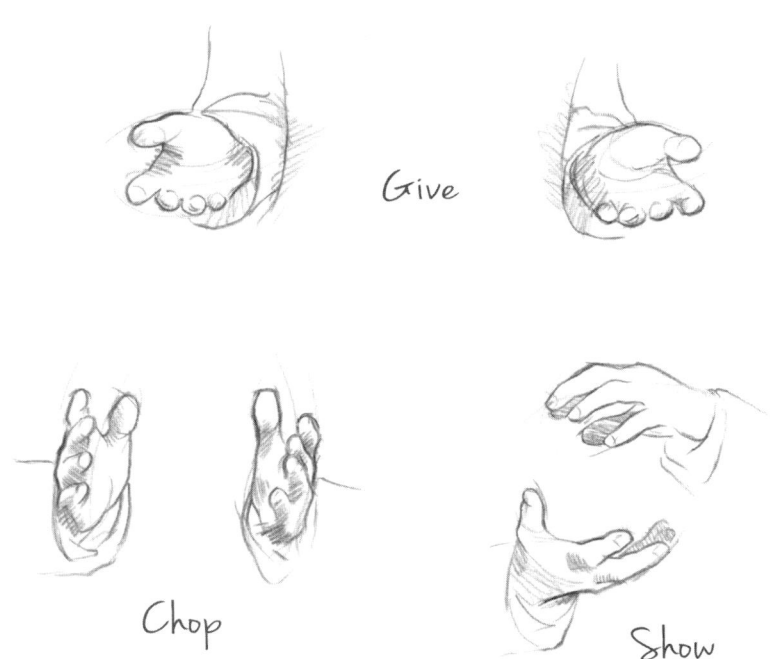

This illustration is from your point of view:

Give. When you give the listener a fact or an argument, the hand appears to engage in the action of giving. The hand is open, with the palm facing upwards. Fingers are straightened and separated slightly, neither tensely squashed together nor splayed widely apart. Look at your own hand and do this palm-up gesture now. Use the *give* gesture and say:

Mr. Douma got to work at 8:30.

This gesture can be done with one or both hands, whether standing or sitting. The *give* gesture is especially useful in court because it is how people gesture when asking questions. When used with a question it becomes the *questioning gesture*. You appear to literally hand the question to the witness just as you would hand her a small object placed on your palm. Try the palms-up *questioning gesture* with both hands and shrug your shoulders slightly. It is clear you are implying a question even if you don't say a word; this is universally understood body language. Use the *give* gesture and ask:

What time did you get to work that day?

Chop. When people speak and gesture emphatically, they turn their hands sideways as if using a gentle karate chop. This gesture is especially useful in closing argument or when asking important leading questions on cross examination. The *chop* gesture accompanies and intensifies a powerful verbal statement. This emphatic *chop* can be done with one or both hands. Hands are usually separated about body-width apart.

When the hands are separated even wider than that, the *chop* is big, powerful, and authoritatively emphatic. Use the *chop* gesture and say:

The defendant's product infringes the patent!

If you find yourself repetitively pointing at the judge, jury, or witness, simply convert your pointing finger to the *chop*.

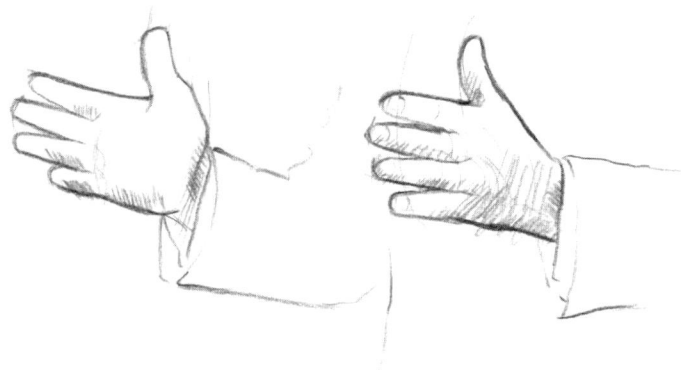

Uncurl and straighten the other four fingers. This turns your pointing finger into the chopping hand of emphasis. No one takes offense if all five fingers are pointing together; it is the index finger alone that is bothersome.

Show. The *show* gesture is sometimes a literal enactment of your words. As you speak, the hands recreate the literal action:

> As he approached the intersection, his left hand held the wheel and his right hand held his phone.

Like a visual aid, the hands *show* or demonstrate what the words are describing, as in this illustration:

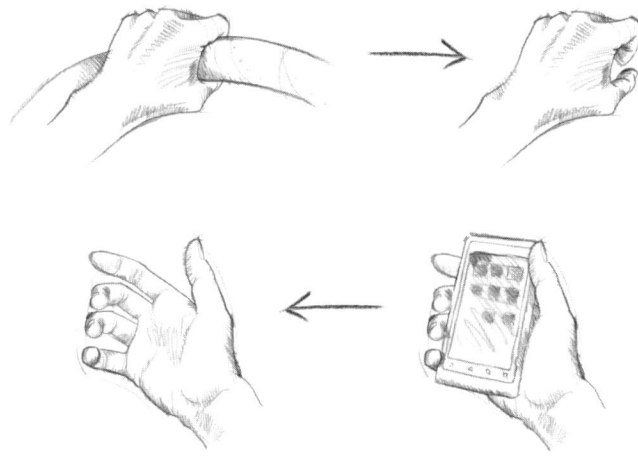

Read that statement aloud and execute the mechanics of the gesture with your own hands to get a feel for this idea. You gesture like this unconsciously all the time.

Sometimes the *show* gesture illustrates a concept, yet still functions as a visual aid for the listener. This sort of expression is common in conversation:

> On the one hand, I'd like to go. On the other hand, I'm too busy.

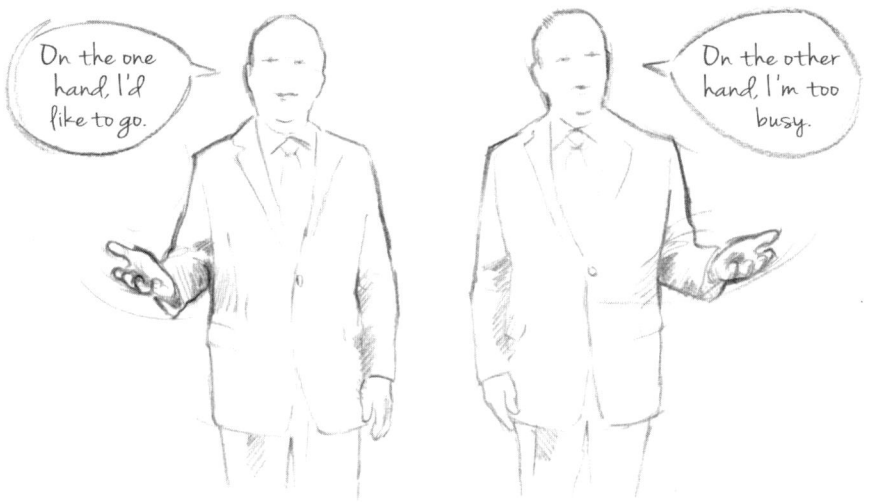

Each gesture *shows* the listener what we are talking about—in this case, the contrast between ideas. In conversation, the listener might well respond, "I see your dilemma." Gestures literally *show* a visualization that the listener sees. Try it. Use your hands to illustrate this issue:

> The invention is neither new (on the one hand) nor novel (on the other hand).

Get the feel for *show* with, "The car came within inches of hitting her," as in this illustration:

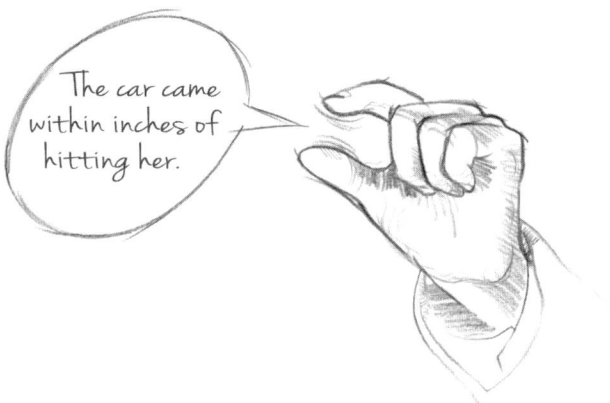

These three choices can trigger your instinct to gesture. Don't be surprised if initially it feels awkward to use *give, chop,* and *show* consciously. It takes practice to get the feel of using them. Use the Three Rs (*ready, release,* and *relax*) and the three gestures (*give, chop,* and *show*) to simplify the challenge of gesturing consciously. One last concept completes your gestural vocabulary.

Gesture "On the Shelf"

A useful method for understanding and jump-starting gestures is to imagine placing ideas "on the shelf." This "shelf" is the bottom of the zone of gesture extending from waist to nose, where the vast majority of natural gestures take place. Therefore, every time you stand up to speak, there is an imaginary, invisible shelf right in front of you. When your hands are in the ready position, they "rest" on this invisible shelf. It is always there, demarcating the bottom of your zone of gesture. When you observe conversational gestures, notice that they usually happen at about waist height—on the shelf—even when people are sitting down.

Whether you *give*, *chop*, or *show*, use the shelf to help jump-start your gestures. For example, giving a question to a witness looks something like the action of placing a big fish on the shelf with both hands.

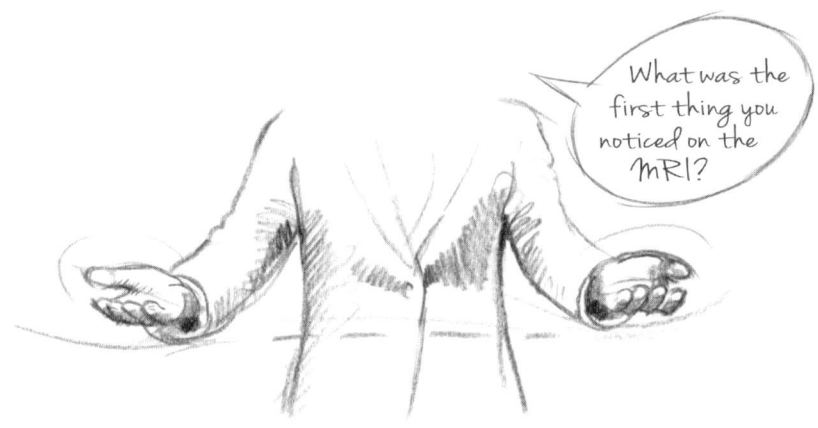

Put the question on the shelf

You can also put the question on the shelf with one hand or the other for variety. Put this book down and make the two-handed give gesture right in front of your seated body at about waist height. Then do it with one hand, and then the other. Gesture while saying aloud:

Where were you on July 4th?

Make it smooth by extending your hands forward as you say "Where," and leave them extended until you say "July 4th." *Give* the whole question from start to finish.

During the emphatic *chop* gesture, the invisible shelf is where a martial artist might break a board with a karate chop. Of course, you will not use the chop with such violence, but the chop happens on the waist-height shelf. If you were a prosecutor speaking to a jury, you might say, "The defendant's *fingerprints* were on the gun." Say it aloud as if you believe it, with a chop gesture on the words *fingerprints* and *gun*.

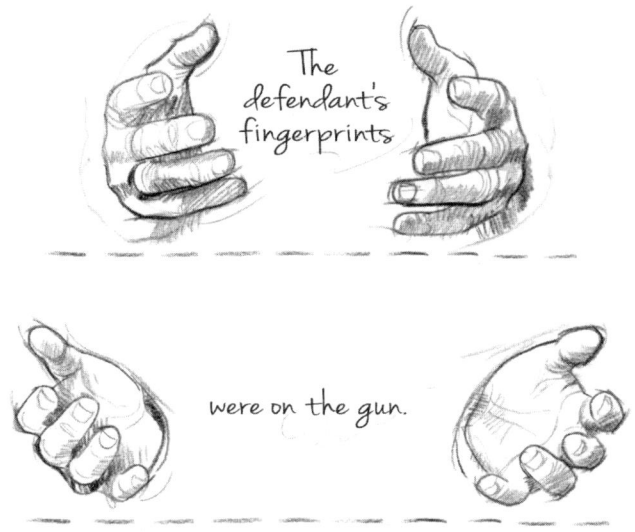

Finally, the *show* gesture places ideas on this same shelf:

Right now, practice several times to get the feel of it.

Some Gestures are Distracting

Everyone has seen speakers whose gestures are distracting and even annoying. Distracting gestures differ fundamentally from natural gestures that are useful and effective.

Repetitive gestures become monotonous and call attention to themselves. If you use the same gesture over and over, it becomes distracting. Such gestures merely keep beating tedious time in an annoying accompaniment to your verbal delivery. "Baton gestures," as they are called, make the speaker look like the mediocre conductor of an inept marching band. Avoid falling into such a gestural rut.

Do not point at your listener with your index finger; it looks like you are nagging rather than persuading. Refrain from pointing repeatedly at the opposing party. Avoid the "thumb puppet," so popular among politicians, where the tip of the thumb sticks up over the index finger of a loose fist. Your credibility will not be enhanced if you look like a politician.

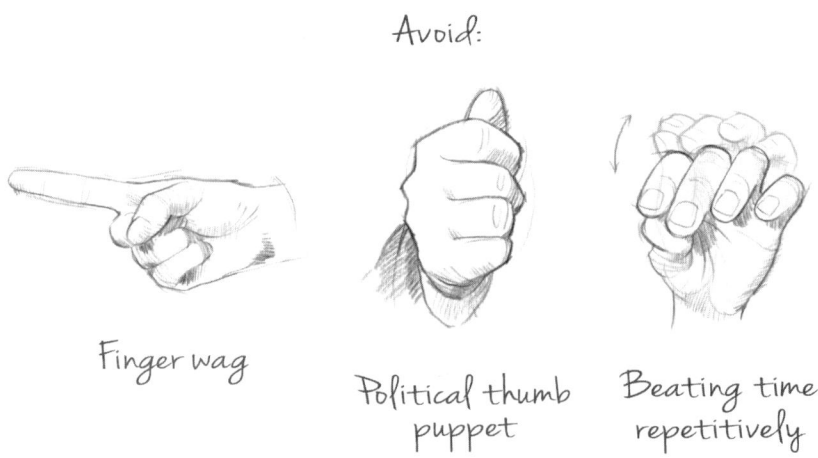

Avoid:

Finger wag   Political thumb puppet   Beating time repetitively

Trust that your natural gestures are not repetitive and monotonous. They are varied because they are inextricably connected to your words.

Don't Hold a Pen

A surprising number of advocates claim to feel more comfortable when they hold a pen while speaking. Why does a slender cylinder of plastic inspire such comfort and confidence? Holding a pen while speaking is illogical. It makes as much sense as holding a microphone while writing. Yet, silly as it is, holding a pen is a widely popular solution to the problem of what to do with your hands.

Obviously, if you need to write something down, pick up your pen and use it, but then put it down. A pen is for writing, not speaking. If you hold a pen you will inevitably distract your listeners with it. You will click it, fondle it, twirl it, and stroke it. Your unconscious fidgeting will prevent your gestures from flowing. The energy of adrenaline will animate your hands to play with your pen and annoy your listeners.

What is the real reason that lawyers like to hold pens? It puts the hands into the ready position! Speakers hold pens with both hands at waist height. So keep the ready position, but get rid of the pen. The same applies to holding anything in your hands—marker pens, a computer remote control, laser pointers, and eyeglasses. If you need a security blanket to hold onto, try the secret handshake instead. Put everything else down.

Summing Up Gestures

Your physical ritual prepares you to gesture. As you adopt your stance, center your body, take a tactical breath, and before you speak, place your hands in the ready position. Immediately upon speaking, jump-start your instinct to gesture using *give, chop,* or *show* gestures, and place them on the shelf. Extend your arms so you have some "air in the armpits." This will help you find gestures that are slower, smoother, larger, and longer. You now have an answer to the question of what to do with your hands. Practice until it becomes second nature.

Posture and Alignment

Moving up the body, posture is the next topic. What is good posture? *Posture* refers to the position or bearing of the body. We can all conjure in our mind's eye a vision of ideal posture: the body upright and erect, the head held high. Imagine an athlete poised for action, a dancer standing on a stage, or a line of soldiers at ease.

Surprisingly, the conventional wisdom you may have learned about how you achieve this proper posture is wrong. Slouching children are told to put their shoulders back and their chests out. But carrying tension in the shoulders and chest doesn't look or feel good. Instead, you look and feel tense because you are tensing the muscles of your upper torso. It is also difficult to maintain this so-called good posture, because it is downright uncomfortable.

Good posture comes from properly aligning your back, chest, shoulders, neck, and head. Your entire spine—which extends from your tailbone up into your skull—must be aligned to gracefully carry the torso, neck, and head over the hips and legs. Good posture includes much more than just your shoulders and chest.

The misguided instruction to pull the shoulders back and thrust the chest up is a response to a real and visible problem. Bad posture appears to be caused by the shoulders slouching forward, which makes the chest collapse. But the real problem begins above the shoulders and chest with the incorrect position of the neck and head.

Your Neck and Head

When you think about your own body, do you imagine that the back of your head shares the same plane as the back of your torso? If you could see yourself in profile, chances are that you would discover that your head and neck are positioned forward of your torso. Because you only see the front view of yourself in mirrors, you may be surprised at how far in front of your body you carry your head and neck (that is, unless you studied ballet for years or have recently served in the military!). People with very poor posture have necks that angle out from the shoulders at 45 degrees, with the head perched way out ahead of the torso. When you watch a crowd of people parade past you, observe this phenomenon. The head leads and the body follows. In contrast, look at very young children; their necks are straight and their heads sit right atop their torsos where they belong.

When your head and neck are too far forward, your shoulders inevitably slouch and your chest collapses. The "shoulders back/chest up" instruction seems to make sense. But collapsed shoulders and chest result from the head and neck being out of alignment. Putting your shoulders back and your chest up does not pull your head and neck back into proper alignment. The best solution is to realign your head and neck so they are properly balanced atop your torso. This repositions your shoulders and chest properly and eliminates nervous tension.

Align Your Spine

Dancers and stage actors are taught to think of good posture as a *direction* to feel and not a *position* to hold. The direction is *upward*, starting from the top of the head. Imagine a bungee cord is attached there. The bungee cord pulls gently upward. As your head pulls up, your neck straightens and lengthens. You neither lift nor tuck your chin as this gentle upward pull occurs. Your face stays on its natural plane, facing forward. When your head and neck move upward, your shoulders and chest move into proper alignment.

You can feel this sensation even while sitting down reading this book. Imagine a gentle force pulling your head upward while lengthening and straightening your neck. Try it. To find the proper place for your shoulders, raise them up toward your ears and then gently drop them back down. Do this several times to relax your shoulder muscles. You needn't lock your shoulders backward with any tension at all because your spine can carry the shoulders effortlessly. Once your head is back on top of—rather than out in front of—your torso, you will look taller and have better posture. Stand up now, and retain that alignment.

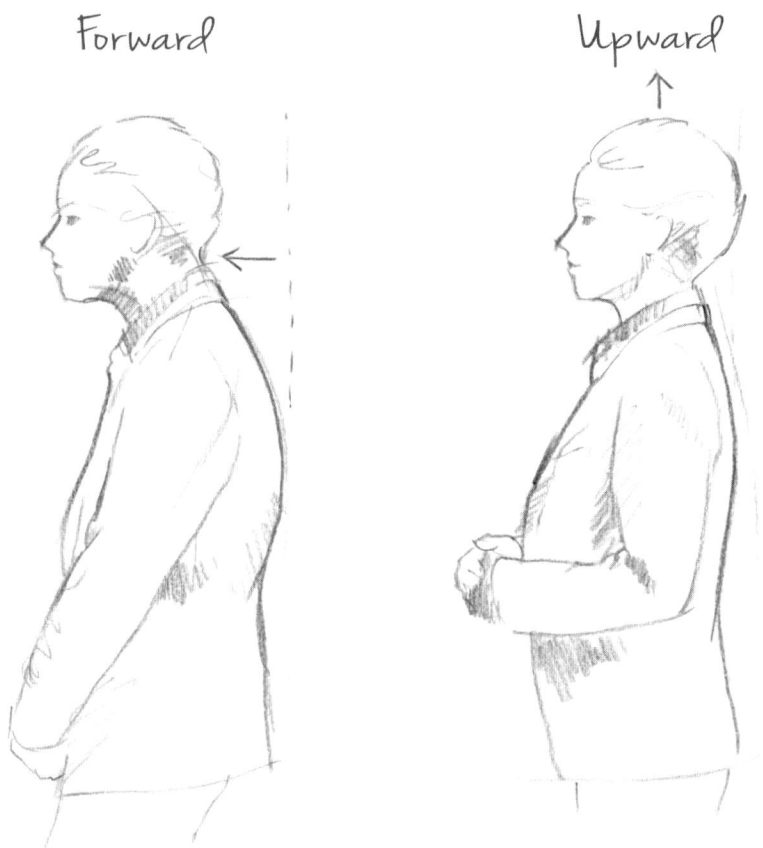

Advocating While Sitting

In some jurisdictions or during arbitrations, you will be required to speak while sitting down. Take care that you think about your body position as you sit, just as you do while standing. Follow these rules:

- Lengthen your spine. Sit up straight and do not slouch.
- Place both feet on the floor.
- Sit on the edge of your seat while speaking.
- Do not lean forward, resting your weight on your elbows.
- Liberate your gestures, and be aware that the zone of gesture may be smaller.
- Speak louder rather than lean in toward a microphone.

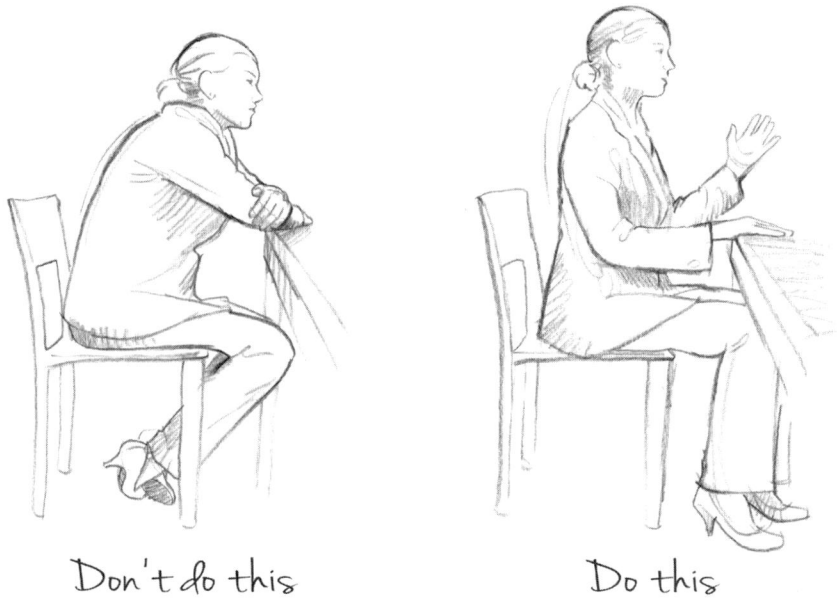

Don't do this   Do this

Your physical ritual now includes your feet, legs, breath, arms, shoulders, back, neck, and head. With your head sitting properly atop your spine, let's explore the challenge of making eye contact. Think about faces.

Your Face

People do not notice gestures because they are not looking at hands and arms. They focus instead on faces and, as they listen, most especially on eyes. Because the listener is focused on your face, you must be aware of your demeanor as you speak.

Your awareness of your face is based almost exclusively on what you see in the mirror. That reflection is not really how it looks to anyone else; it is a backward mirror image. The left side of your face appears to be the right side and vice versa. Perhaps this is one reason why video is so unnerving. It shows your face as it really appears, with the right side on the right side; you aren't used to seeing that image. When you look in a mirror you are not conversing, arguing, or questioning. You are passively regarding your face. That passivity may lead you to a distorted view of yourself and your natural facial animation.

During advocacy training, lawyers watching themselves on video often say, "I make all these weird expressions with my face!" But those expressions do not look odd to the rest of the world. The facial animation you may see as unnatural on video is what other people see all the time. As with all elements of physical style, your face should do what it naturally does. To achieve this goal, become more aware of your own facial animation and expressions.

Your Mouth

Consider your mouth and lips. It is common for people under pressure to reveal their anxiety by tensing their lips. Some people press their lips tightly together. Others tuck one lip inside and gently chew on it. This tension looks peculiar. Instead, your face should look at ease and comfortable with no visible tension, a look best described as "neutral alert." In neutral alert you appear attentive without revealing obvious emotion; you are neither smiling nor frowning. To achieve neutral alert, part your lips slightly—no more than a quarter of an inch—and breathe through both your mouth and nose. When your lips are slightly parted, they cannot tense, scowl, or tuck.

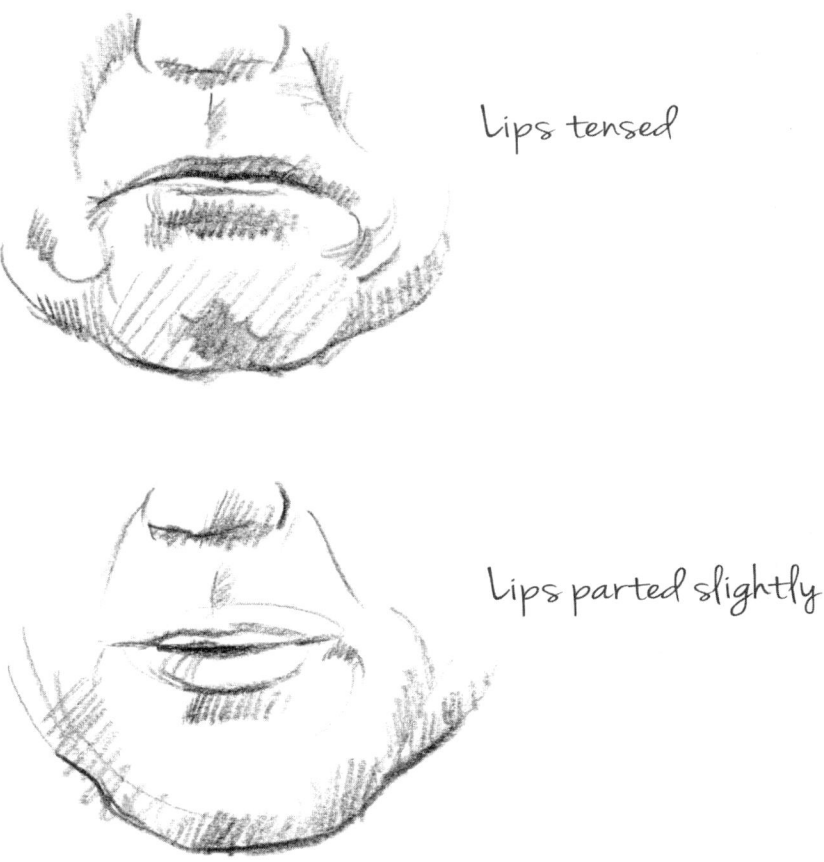

Lips tensed

Lips parted slightly

If your mouth naturally turns down in an unintended frown, be especially aware of maintaining neutral alert. Otherwise you may appear to be frowning and scowling at your own witnesses. Parting the lips slightly makes the frown disappear.

Your Furrowed Brow

Another area of potential tension is the forehead and brow. When people concentrate, they often tense the muscles in the upper part of the face, above and between the eyebrows. This furrowed brow of concentration can make you seem angry and annoyed. Use your physical ritual to become aware of what your forehead is doing. Be sure to include your face and eyes in your mnemonic ritual checklist—that way you will avoid making a scowling, negative first impression.

Lift and relax your brow

    A furrowed brow results from tension in the forehead that draws the eyebrows together. To fix the problem, gently move the muscles in your forehead in opposite directions. When you lift your eyebrows slightly, the tension disappears. Lift your brows whenever you sense that your forehead and brows are tense. Look in a mirror to see this subtle effect. By moving your mouth and your forehead slightly, your face looks alert yet neutral—neither scowling nor artificially happy.

Eye Contact

Everyone knows that eye contact is important. It's as true of personal conversations as it is when speaking to a judge, jury, or arbitrator. Ultimately, credibility hinges on the answer to this question: "Can you look me in the eye as you tell me that?" If you don't look fact finders in the eye, you won't be credible.

Eye contact is also an important element of listening. When a witness is answering your questions, you need to consciously *listen with your eyes* and focus on her to make sure you hear what she is saying. The same thing applies when a judge is asking you questions. If your eyes are focused on your notes instead of the speaker, you will inevitably miss something important. The brain cannot simultaneously read notes and listen attentively.

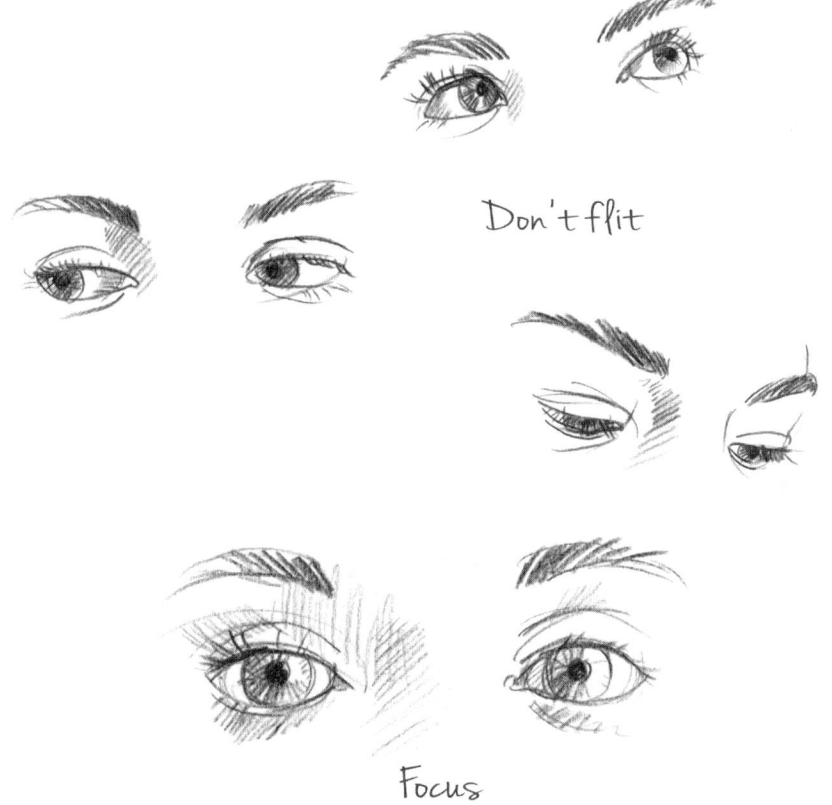

Finally, you must focus your eyes and focus your brain to be able to think effectively on your feet. You can't focus your brain if you don't focus your eyes. This idea is developed further in the chapter about the brain, but it is useful to consider the issue as it affects your eyes.

Even though you *know* you should look people in the eye, making eye contact can be surprisingly difficult when speaking under pressure. There are two reasons for this difficulty. First, everyone has a personal mannerism that dictates where the eyes focus while thinking. Some people think while casting their eyes up to the ceiling; others look at the floor to think, while still others look off to the side. These mannerisms do not need to be eliminated, but they must be controlled. If your eyes flit up to the ceiling as you cast about for the next word or phrase, don't stare at the ceiling for too long. Raise your awareness of your own mannerism and control it. If your eyes break contact briefly, it's not a big problem. But if your eyes appear to linger on the ceiling, floor, or wall for too long, you will look distracted, absent-minded, or simply stumped. The secret to eye contact is to keep returning the focus to people, not things.

Follow this simple rule: never begin speaking until your eyes are focused on another person. When examining a witness, don't say a word until you have lifted your eyes up and out of your notes and focused on the person on the stand. Resist the powerful temptation to begin speaking while your eyes are still focused on your notes. Talk to people, not paper.

Another factor that makes eye contact challenging is the stoic facial expressions of listeners in legal proceedings. In conversation, you get regular, subtle feedback from people. They nod, raise their eyebrows, smile, frown, and make those reassuring noises that indicate they are listening. We expect and need some type of physical and/or verbal indication that we are being listened to. Yet when you are speaking to a judge, jury, or arbitrator, almost all of that feedback vanishes.

Stone-faced jurors offer few clues about what they are thinking. If a friend or colleague looked at you with such an indifferent expression you would probably ask, "What's wrong? Why is he looking at me like that?"

You may find these stoic expressions intimidating and distracting, yet they are natural for jurors listening to you. It is not their job to telegraph their responses with nods, smiles, or frowns. Thankfully, some jurors may provide limited physical responses, and an advocate's eyes tend to gravitate to those people. But generally jurors sit poker-faced. They may look unfriendly, even hostile. Don't let this throw you. Your job is to make eye contact with all the jurors, no matter how difficult this sometimes may be. You can't judge a book by its cover.

You can't judge listeners by their expressions

One reason eye contact is challenging has to do with our old friend adrenaline. In his book *Complications: A Surgeon's Notes on an Imperfect Science*, Dr. Atul Gawande writes about a scientific examination of extreme facial blushing under the pressure of performance:

> *In an odd experiment conducted a couple of years ago, two social psychologists ... wired subjects with facial temperature sensors and put them on one side of a one-way mirror. The mirror was then removed to reveal an entire audience staring at them from the other side. Half the time the audience members were wearing dark glasses, and half the time, they were not. Strangely, subjects blushed only when they could see the audience's eyes.*

Psychologists studying the causes of blushing had uncovered a physiological change in the body triggered by eye contact alone. Performance pressure (speaking to audiences or juries) triggers adrenaline flow, increases blood pressure, and—for some speakers—can cause intense blushing of the face and neck. It is especially apparent at the beginning of a presentation, when the audience is most focused on the speaker. But these subjects were not even required to speak; they merely had to stand in silence while being stared at by all those eyes. Eye contact alone increased adrenaline flow, blood pressure, and facial temperature. When the sunglasses blocked eye contact, the subjects did not blush.

Being stared at by a group triggers a predator–prey response and the fight-or-flight response of adrenaline. This physiological response to the gaze of others may help explain why so many speakers find it difficult to sustain eye contact with listeners, even when they know they should.

Despite the physiological challenge of eye contact, you can control where you focus your eyes. Look at listeners individually and repeatedly, even those with the most unresponsive expressions. Sustained eye contact will enhance your credibility and help you concentrate on a witness's answers, a judge's question, or any critical exchange in any forum.

Use this simple technique to get your eyes under your control. During those few seconds of silence before you utter a word, look at the perimeter of your audience and make eye contact with the people at the four corners: front row, far right; back row, far right; back row, far left; front row, far left. Within that target area are all the eyes you want to contact. If you stake out the perimeter of your audience, you will help your brain see everyone sitting before you.

How long should you make contact? Here's an analogy for the proper duration of eye contact. Imagine you are watering a garden, and your goal is to water every plant in the garden evenly. You sweep the hose back and forth across the garden plants randomly. You don't want to soak just one plant, washing away the soil from its roots, but to water every plant equally. Similarly, when you look at the audience, look at them all regularly and consistently. You may linger on each pair of eyes for only a second or two, but you can create the feeling that you are talking to them all individually, all the time.

A discussion earlier in this chapter urged you to avoid random pacing. Pacing distracts listeners and requires them to follow meaningless movement around the room. But pacing also robs them of eye contact. One of the liabilities of pacing back and forth in front of your listeners is that you can't make consistent eye contact with everyone. As you move to one side, the folks on the opposite side see your backside and not your eyes. When you move in the opposite direction, the other side is deprived of eye contact. So stand still most of the time and let your eyes move back and forth and up and down, randomly making eye contact.

Eyes and Notes

When you need to look at your notes, don't be afraid to stop and read. Listeners don't mind if you look at your notes occasionally, but they do mind if you *talk* to your notes. If you stand up and read a script word for word, your listeners will be very poorly served. (Chapter Two discusses notes in detail.) Fact finders don't like to be read to, but they do expect that a lawyer will periodically look at notes. So when you do, don't rush. Stop and read. Look down long enough to see where you are and establish what you want to say next. Then bring your eyes back up, focus on a human being, and begin speaking again.

Summary

To master the challenge of controlling and coordinating your body as an advocate, you must cope with both your conscious and unconscious behaviors while under pressure. Sometimes you will deliberately jump-start instinctive behaviors, such as natural gesturing. Other times your conscious brain helps to prevent unconscious behaviors, such as nervous fidgeting or pacing. Simply telling yourself to be natural will not work.

Adrenaline is a natural source of energy, but it can be a nuisance unless you understand and channel it. Be prepared to cope with it each time you make a presentation. Realize that adrenaline can make your legs, arms, hands, and voice tremble.

Breathe consciously, using tactical breathing to control the volume of your voice and to calm yourself. Find and release your own natural instinct to gesture, making sure you have a technique for jump-starting your gestures at the beginning of each presentation. Pay attention to your body's alignment. Release tension in your face, and make eye contact with the fact finder.

Develop a physical ritual you will use each time you speak. Practice your physical ritual until it becomes second nature.

Talk to Yourself

"Take deep, slow breaths while waiting to stand and speak."

"Don't speak until you plant your feet and calmly inhale."

"Look at all of them before speaking."

"Part your lips slightly to relax your face."

"Raise your hands to the ready position and gesture immediately."

"Jump-start gestures and put some opening words on the shelf."

"Gesture slowly and smoothly to start and feel more natural."

"Give away nervousness with the *give* gesture."

Chapter Two
Your Brain

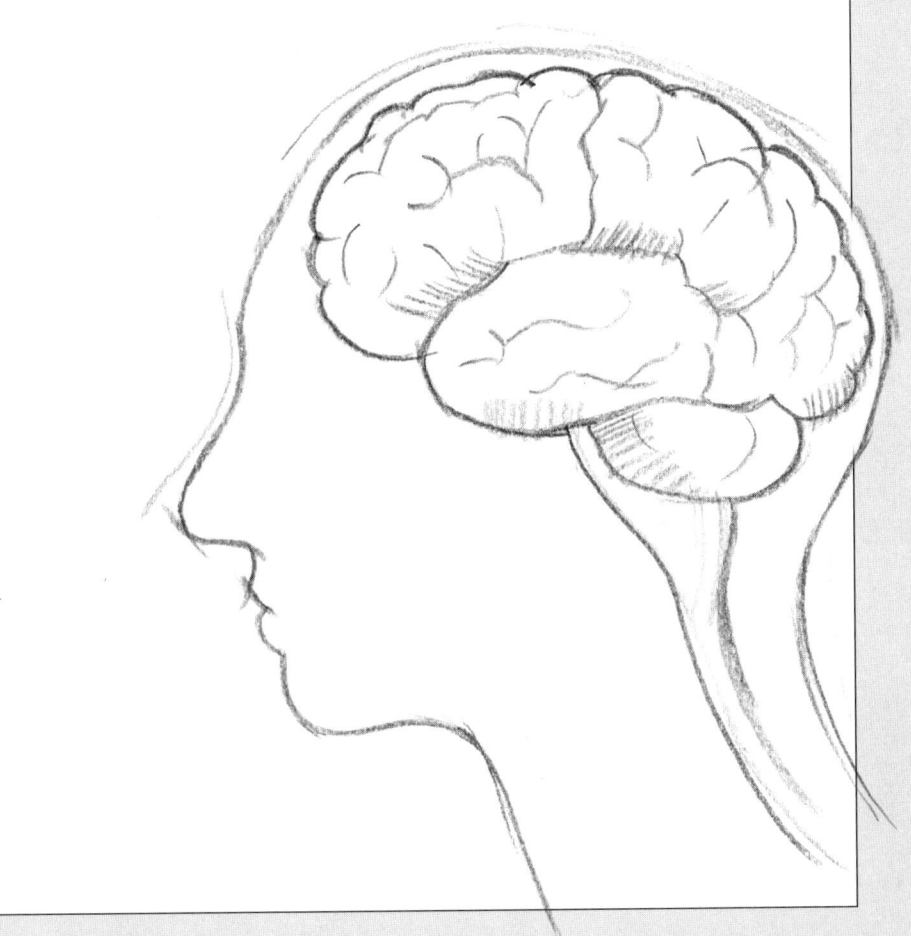

Adrenaline profoundly affects your brain as well as your muscles. It is imperative that you understand the impact it has on your cognitive processes—and that you learn how to control and channel its power.

Adrenaline alters how you experience the passage of time. This can help, or hinder, your ability to function as an advocate, as well as your effectiveness in speaking clearly and persuasively under pressure. Adrenaline can be an enemy, making you more nervous and causing you to speak too quickly, or it might befriend you, creating the sense that you have plenty of time to contemplate what to say.

Perhaps you've noticed that most public speakers talk too quickly when they get nervous. This happens when adrenaline flows to a speaker's brain. It creates the illusion of a time warp; time seems to pass more slowly. To compensate, speakers often accelerate the pace of their speech, but talking too fast makes thinking much more difficult for both the speaker and listener. When you're under pressure, you need extra time to gather and process your thoughts. Adrenaline can help.

Adrenaline and the Time Warp

Induced by a rush of adrenaline, the time warp is a vital complement to the fight-or-flight energy sent to your muscles. When threatened, you must decide whether to stand your ground and fight, or turn on your heels and flee. It would be ideal if you had lots of time to weigh your options and make the right choice when making a life-or-death decision. But you don't have the luxury of time; you must respond instantly to a perceived threat. In this moment of crisis, adrenaline helps you make the right decision by altering your perception of time's passage. It seems to expand the moment, enabling you to weigh your options and make the best choice. You may have experienced this phenomenon if you have ever genuinely feared for your life.

Consider this scenario: You are driving down the street toward an intersection. The light is green. Being a defensive driver, you glance left and then right as you approach to make certain that no vehicle is running the red. Suddenly, there it is! A big green garbage truck is barreling down on the red light, headed for your driver's-side door. You've got three seconds to save yourself. You think, "*I'm about to die!*" If you have survived such a moment, you'll recall the feeling of time slowing down. Survivors' accounts of their experiences are consistent: "When I saw that garbage truck, I thought I was going to die! And everything slowed way down." They frequently add: "At that moment, my whole life flashed before me!" How, in three seconds, can there be time for your whole life to flash before you? That detailed historical review of your existence occurs as your brain is simultaneously weighing a number of complex alternatives:

Swerve left? No, oncoming traffic!
Swerve right? No, little kids on the sidewalk!
Slam on the brakes? Too late for that!
Speed up? Yes, floor it!

Although scientists cannot fully explain how the time warp works, it's thanks to adrenaline that the brain seemingly has extra time to perform all those complex calculations (involving speed, mass, distance, and even ethics) necessary to assure your safety.

The human experience of time is highly subjective. In everyday life, time appears to pass much faster or slower depending on your circumstances. When you're having a good time, time seems to fly by. If you're bored and watching the clock, time slows to a crawl. Of course, the actual passage of time never really changes: a second lasts one second, a minute lasts one minute, an hour takes an hour.

Your subjective experience of time's passage, whether faster or slower, is also influenced by how much information your brain is processing in any given moment. During an adrenaline rush, as you instantly analyze and respond to a perceived threat, your brain processes information at an unusually high rate. In his classic book *On the Experience of Time*, Robert E. Ornstein refers to studies that found that "the amount of mental content in an interval determines its subjective duration." In other words, if your brain is processing increased amounts of information, as it must in a life-or-death situation (or while advocating), you may subjectively experience time as slowing down.

Another theory involves heart rate and adrenaline. Ornstein refers to a study showing that "with more 'beats' in an interval, time experience lengthens." Your resting heart rate is about 60 beats per minute. The regular rhythmic tempo of everyday life is *one heartbeat = one second*. Under the influence of adrenaline, however, your heart rate accelerates dramatically to 120 beats per minute or more. Your brain registers twice as many heartbeats per minute, and therefore twice as many "seconds" appear to pass in a given interval.

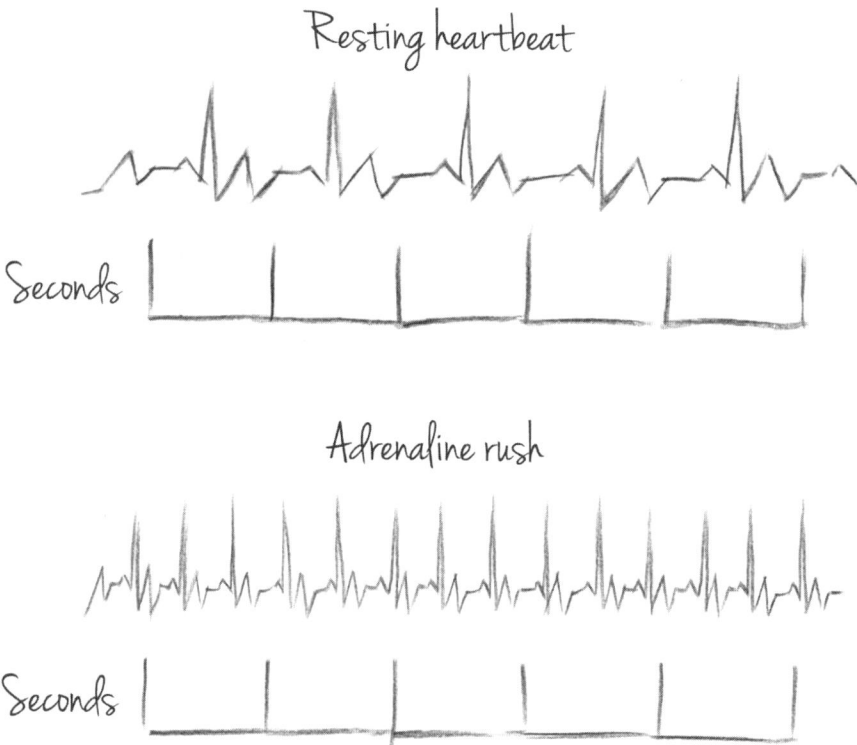

Paradoxically, time seems to slow down as your heart rate speeds up.

As an advocate, you can turn the subjectivity of time's passing to your advantage. Make it part of your technique; train yourself to channel and exploit the time warp. Rather than allowing it to prompt you to speak faster, use the time warp to give yourself the sense that you have more time to think. Instead of your whole life passing before you, now all available thoughts and words will flash in front of you.

Seeking the Zone of Concentration

Being "pumped," as athletes are in competition, involves both muscles and mind. Muscles are highly energized, the mind sharply focused. Athletes who learn to exploit the benefits of the time warp refer to this heightened state of concentration as being "in the zone." While in this zone of concentration, an athlete has more time to make decisions concerning the right moves to execute in order to play the game successfully. The great home-run slugger Ted Williams famously exploited the time warp in the batter's box. Being in the zone of concentration allowed him plenty of time to decide whether, and how, to swing at a pitch. Tennis legend Roger Federer has described having a leisurely amount of time to return a ball that appears large and slow as it leaves an opponent's racquet. Solo climber Peter Croft describes clarity and near-supernatural concentration when scaling a rock face without a rope.

For an advocate experiencing the time warp, silence can be particularly uncomfortable and intimidating. Time appears to pass so slowly that a silence of almost any length seems oppressively long, especially at the beginning of a presentation, when the initial adrenaline rush is most intense.

To compensate for these "long" silences, nervous advocates often rush to fill the void with thinking noises—*uh* and *um*—and they talk too fast. This sets a tempo that is impossible to sustain. Talking fast may fill the silence, but it also eliminates your thinking time. As a result, your brain cannot formulate clear, concise sentences or questions. Even if you could speak articulately at a fast pace, judges, jurors, witnesses, and court reporters couldn't keep up with you. Although your words might be understood, their meaning is not. For the listener, words spoken too quickly go in one ear and out the other. You cannot be persuasive when your tongue races. Moments of silence are a gift of adrenaline's time warp. Use them.

As it does for athletes in the almost magical zone of concentration, adrenaline's time warp can work for you instead of against you. When you exploit the time warp, your silences will still feel much longer than normal—but in a good and useful way. With practice, the time warp will afford you what feels like an extra-long interval to consider what you want to say. Those three seconds of silence may feel like twelve. What a luxury to have so much apparent time to think! You've got all the time you need to choose the right word or formulate your next sentence. You can weigh the merits of ending a line of questioning or delving more deeply into a topic. You have time to choose your next word, respond to an objection, or answer a judge's question. Silence becomes a valuable tool, an important part of your technique.

Become aware of the silence in the room *before* you start to speak. When you first stand up, don't say anything. Pause for a few seconds, and count silently to yourself: one-thousand-one, one-thousand-two, one-thousand-three. It will seem like a long time, but it isn't. Purposefully focus on hearing the silence in the room. Once you've heard it, use it when you speak. Weave short, one-second gaps into your delivery. Say a phrase and stop (silence); say another phrase and stop (silence). At the end of a sentence, and especially at the end of a topic or line of questioning, pause even longer and listen. During that silence—think! You will find that once you begin to focus on silence and its intersection with speech, you will grow comfortable using it.

Exploiting the time warp and its partner, silence, enhances your capacity to think and speak effectively. It also increases the listener's capacity to understand and be persuaded by what you have to say. Silence is a critical component of the thought process. Listeners need time to think. If you want to persuade people, you need to give them time to reflect. They aren't persuaded by what you say *as* you are saying it; they are persuaded when they have a moment of silence to think about what you just said.

Consider the thought process of your listeners, whether they are judges or arbitrators, and especially if they are jurors. They are not trained, as you are, to think like a lawyer. One of the challenges of being a juror is to get comfortable with legal issues, legal jargon, and legal concepts. It's foreign territory, cognitively speaking. Jurors need more time than you do to think through what is being said—to grasp your meaning fully and, ultimately, to be persuaded. It is only *after* you have spoken that the jury has time to consider your words. The amount of time you require to choose your words is certainly less than the amount of time your jurors need to think about what you've just said. Give them time to think and process, and then to form an opinion.

Echo Memory

In the courtroom, judges and jurors use "echo memory." As the word "echo" implies, the brain of an attentive listener is experiencing this phenomenon.

> As you speak ... *As you speak ...*
> the listener's brain ... *the listener's brain ...*
> echoes back what you say ... *echoes back what you say.*

Echo memory is used routinely in everyday life. For example, if you hear a phone number, you may simply say it aloud as a memory aid—*555-1212 ... 555-1212 ... 555-1212*—until you input the number in your smartphone. That repetition, or echoing, helps the brain remember. We do the same thing when getting directions.

During an examination, the echo memory in a fact finder's brain might be represented as such:

Q: What do you do for a living?
A: I'm a general contractor.
Fact finder: (*Oh, he's a general contractor.*)

Students taking notes while listening to a professor's lecture are engaged in a version of echo memory. They echo into their laptops or their notebooks the important ideas the professor says. If she speaks too quickly, however, the students are unable to take notes effectively. Whether the listeners are students taking notes or jurors simply taking note of what you are saying, they need time to let your thoughts sink in. The more complex and/or important the information you give your fact finders, the more time they need to echo it back in their own minds in order to grasp it and be persuaded. When you give your listeners time to think about what you say, you are exploiting *persuasive silence*. Everyone is familiar with the expression "Silence is golden." It is derived from a nineteenth-century saying—"Speech is silver, but silence is golden"—that emphasizes the key role silence plays in communication. Words are important, silence even more so.

Thinking On Your Feet

Once you realize that you need time (and silence) to think on your feet, the next step is to understand exactly *how* to think on your feet. Should you read? What about memorization? Can you write out what you want to say? What's the problem with reading or reciting?

Do Not Read

Do not read from your notes. Reading is deadly. You may be tempted to do so, thinking that it will increase the chance that your delivery will be perfect. But the only perfection you will achieve is to be perfectly boring! It is unlikely that you have been trained, as broadcasters and actors are, to read aloud skillfully. Reading aloud is an art unto itself, and many actors can't even do it well. Every year at the Academy Awards, renowned actors struggle to read a few lines off a teleprompter.

Everyone makes the same mistakes when reading aloud. You read too fast. You read without natural expression and inflection, burying your nose in your notes. If you decide to read during a legal proceeding, you will rarely look your listeners in the eye, and you will lack credibility. You will sound and look like you are reading—because you are! Listeners are not fooled by reading. If you wish to persuade people, you mustn't *read at* them, you must *talk to* them.

During examinations, resist the temptation to read from your notes as you ask questions. You do not possess the gift of prophecy. While preparing for a trial, you cannot predict what a witness will say. This is true even during direct examination with a well-prepared witness. People are unpredictable, especially when performing under pressure and feeling nervous. Reading a list of written questions presupposes that the examiner knows the exact words the witness will use to answer each question. Here is an example of what can happen if advocates bury their eyes in notes and simply read the questions. This advocate wasn't listening, and so didn't expect the second part of each answer:

> Q: Ms. Hernandez, tell us where you live.
> A: I live in San Diego with my husband.
> Q: Are you married?
> A: Yes, with two kids.
> Q: Do you have any children?
> A: Yes, a boy, 6, and a girl, 8.
> Q: What are their ages?

As silly as that sounds, it is a common and comical occurrence at trial advocacy training programs. The advocate incorrectly assumes that the witness will give precisely the answer imagined. The extra detail provided with each answer was not anticipated. The problem is compounded when advocates are so focused on reading the next question from a legal pad that they don't listen to the answers given by the witness. The result is absurd.

Do Not Recite

Recitation—repeating aloud or declaiming a text from memory—is a highly specialized skill. Even with years of training and practice, professional actors in a stage play require weeks of rehearsal to memorize and recite their lines accurately and confidently. As a busy lawyer, you can't spend weeks memorizing your presentations. You're apt to have a memory slip—and a single slip can undermine your confidence. If you can't think of the next word to say, you're stumped. If a critical issue arises after you have painstakingly memorized your opening or closing, it will be challenging to incorporate new facts smoothly. Recitation from memory *sounds* odd to listeners. You look a bit glassy-eyed when reciting, because your mind is elsewhere: on the task of recalling what you wrote. So don't try to memorize and recite your presentations; the risk of error is great.

Since you're not going to read and you're not going to recite, you have only one option left: talk.

Structured Improvisation

The style of thinking you do as an advocate is best described as structured improvisation. In advance, you structure carefully the order of topics you intend to talk about in your motion, appeal, opening, closing, or examinations. Using that structure, you improvise word-by-word, just as you do in conversational speech. Your brain is quite adept at this kind of thinking and speaking.

Suppose you say to a colleague, "We need to talk about yesterday's phone call and tomorrow's meeting." Here is your structure:

1. phone call
2. meeting

Using that two-part structure, you simply talk, improvising the actual words as you go along. As an advocate, you structure longer presentations with more information. Your previous experience with this skill allows you to do it naturally.

Think about a story from your own life that you have told many times—a personal anecdote about something humorous, frightening, or bizarre. If you were asked to tell a listener about that experience, you wouldn't hesitate or struggle, because you lived the story and have told it—in effect, have practiced telling it—many times before. Now imagine that you were asked to tell that same anecdote again to a different listener, immediately, but with one additional, impossible requirement: you must tell it verbatim, word-for-word, exactly as you did the first time.

You couldn't do that. Nobody could. This would not indicate that you suddenly were unable to remember the event. It simply would mean that you could not remember and repeat verbatim the words you used to describe it, although you had uttered that description just minutes before. If you cannot accomplish this task even with a familiar anecdote, you can hardly hope to deliver verbatim a legal presentation that you wrote in the recent past. The brain isn't built that way.

Telling your personal story requires a form of structured improvisation. The sequence of events is the structure; you improvise around it, retelling the anecdote using different words, phrases, and sentences. Structured improvisation also works for examinations. Plan your examinations according to the topic areas you wish to discuss, and then improvise your questions around that structure while listening carefully to the answers you receive.

Advocating with structured improvisation is like performing a kind of verbal jazz. You can learn to be comfortable living in this cognitive state, poised between the opposites of well-planned structure and free-form improvisation. You have to prepare carefully for what you hope and expect will happen. But once you are making an opening statement or examining a witness, you need to deal with what is really happening, which may be different from what you expected. In essence, you train your brain to structure and remember your ideas in a specific order, but not with the precise words you actually will use.

Athletes playing a team sport, such as football, practice the plays they intend to use in a game. Once the game begins, however, the players must improvise if the quarterback fumbles the ball, or the passing play is broken up by the blitzing linebacker, or the pass receiver slips and falls. Advocacy might be described as a verbal game in which similarly unexpected things can and do occur. Just as in a game, there are opposing teams, a judge acting as referee, definite rules governing how the game must be played, and a winner and a loser. As with any athletic competition, advocacy as a verbal battle of wits requires practice and preparation, as well as the ability to improvise, deal with the unexpected, and go with the flow during the game.

Do Not Read and Talk Simultaneously

Your brain is not experienced at talking and reading simultaneously. In everyday life, when you talk, you talk, and when you read, you read. Do not create notes with prose paragraphs that must be read. Such notes are a trap. The more words you write, the less helpful the notes become. When you are speaking to an audience, there just isn't time to read all those words. If you stand up with a lengthy, detailed script, the temptation to read it will be irresistible. As your brain doesn't naturally talk and read at the same time, it must do one or the other. It chooses reading, because that is the safer choice. But reading inevitably is boring.

The written word is processed in a different part of the brain than the spoken word. Functional magnetic resonance imaging, or fMRI, which can "look" into the thinking brain, reveals that reading and speaking happen in two different areas. To attempt to read your notes while talking at the same time is analogous to running two incompatible software programs on your computer. Your brain's cognitive hard drive will crash. So pick the proper cognitive software: talk to your listeners. Reading aloud isn't effective, talking is. And it is what you already do whenever you communicate.

In dissuading you from reading, we don't mean to suggest that you can't have notes to guide your structured improvisation. Listeners expect that a speaker will look at an outline periodically. It's perfectly okay to *look at* your notes, just don't *talk to* them. There's a huge difference, and it's all a matter of timing. The secret of creating useful notes is to conceive of them as a visual aid for yourself.

Notes as Your Visual Aid

Notes are very often a necessity. In a complex case, notes lying on a lectern or counsel table guide you through your speeches or examinations. They help you structure and remember what you want to say and are a comforting security blanket when your mind goes blank.

Truly useful speaking notes serve as visual aids. Fundamentally they differ in purpose and design from the "thinking notes" you jot down initially as you collect your thoughts about a case, and they are distinct from the "listening notes" you write on your legal pad as opposing counsel examines a witness. Additionally, those thinking and listening notes are not big enough—and often not legible enough—to be a good visual aid.

Good visual aids provide a structure around which a speaker can improvise. Here are some rules to help you create good notes for use in the courtroom.

Write big. If you create notes using your computer, double or triple the size of the font, from 10- or 12-point to 24- or 26-point. Make big notes that are easy to read, so that when you glance at them, the words leap off the page. You'll be amazed at how much easier it is to speak with notes you can read easily. They should look something like this:

Write big.
Write legibly.
Keep notes simple.
Keep notes handy.

For handwritten notes, use a pen that makes a fat line on the paper. Big, thick writing can be seen easily, even at a distance. Notes written too small are indecipherable lying on counsel table three or four feet away. Consider the distance your eyes are from the page that you are reading now. If your notes are lying on a lectern twice the distance from your eyes, shouldn't they be written twice as big? If they are lying on counsel table three times the distance from your eyes, shouldn't they be written at least three times as large as regular writing?

Write legibly. Carefully print your notes so that they are legible. It takes a bit more time and effort, but it's well worth it. Key words, dates, or dollar amounts could be printed in red to highlight their importance; emphasize important words with a yellow highlighter. When you write legibly as well as large, it prevents you from putting too many words on a page. That's a good thing, because it reinforces the next rule.

Keep notes simple. Less is more. Fewer words are more useful. Boil down your big ideas to just a few words that will trigger the whole thought. Remember, the more words you put on paper, the less useful the notes become. Avoid prose sentences. Write down the structure of your ideas, then improvise around that structure. Don't waste space writing, "Good morning, members of the jury, my name is …"

Stand back from the lectern

Keep notes handy. Place your notes where you can see them easily. If you are required to speak from behind a lectern, step back about 12 inches—reading your notes should require only a downward shift of your eyes. If you step to the side of the lectern, position yourself so that you can see your notes without moving your feet. Beware of the tendency to step to the side of the lectern and then forward a step or two. That makes it impossible to read your notes without crab-walking backward to glance at them. Stand *still* where you can see your notes, especially if you need to look at them often.

Create horizontal notes. The notes you create for speaking will be much more useful once you recognize the difference between how you *write* versus how you think, speak, and gesture. Simply stated: you write *vertically*, but you think and gesture *horizontally*. With this understanding, you can create notes that synchronize with how your brain remembers and how your hands gesture. Ultimately, this even helps your listeners understand and remember what you said—which is, after all, your purpose.

When you read and write, thoughts and words flow line by line, from top to bottom, down a printed page or a computer screen. Writers explicitly refer to this top-down flow with expressions like "as described above" and "as discussed below." Thinking while reading and writing is about vertical flow from top to bottom.

Thinking while speaking is altogether different. Your ideas and gestures flow back and forth horizontally. This is why using conventional vertical notes can be so unhelpful when you are advocating under pressure.

As proof of your own horizontal thinking, consider the expression "On the one hand … and on the other hand." This gesture pattern is used to compare and contrast, like this:

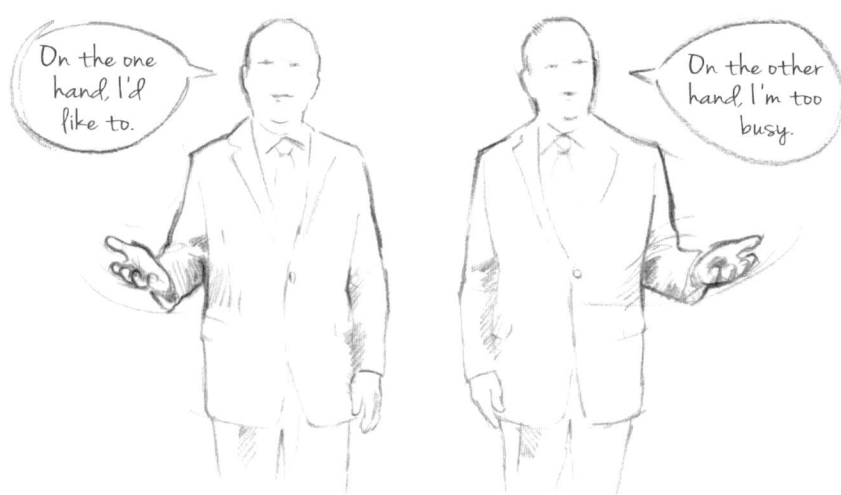

Does anyone ever gesture such a dilemma top to bottom, vertically?

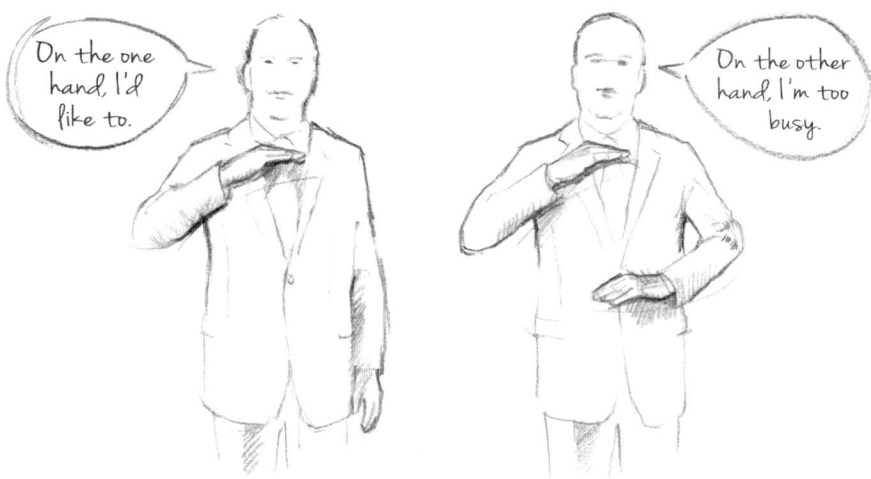

We never do this!

As another example of horizontal thinking, imagine speaking and gesturing about the past, present, and future. How would you logically gesture this personal timeline?

> Yesterday I was at work; today I'm at home; tomorrow I leave on vacation.

You gesture the past, present, and future along a horizontal plane. Notice how peculiar it feels to say this sentence aloud while gesturing vertically from top to bottom:

> Yesterday I was at work;
> today I'm at home;
> tomorrow I leave on vacation.

Recall from Chapter One that the horizontal plane where speakers gesture is called "the shelf." When people gesture unconsciously, their hands appear to be placing words, ideas, and concepts on an invisible shelf in front of them. The shelf is about waist high, and speakers appear to use it whether sitting or standing.

If your brain thinks horizontally, and your hands gesture horizontally on the shelf, it makes sense that your notes should reflect this pattern. Create notes that flow from side to side across a piece of paper. Longer legal pads are especially good for this. You can arrange a substantial amount of information across 14 inches of paper. If using your computer, compose and print with the landscape setting. We use horizontal notes while lecturing on the topics described in this book. Here is an example of our horizontal notes:

Body	Brain	Voice
• Adrenaline	• Adrenaline	• Chunking
• Stand	• Time Warp	• Phrasing
• Breathe	• Silence	• Emphasizing
• Gesture	• Thinking	• Gesturing
• Focus	• Echo Memory	• Punctuation

Notice the second advantage of arranging notes horizontally. It forces one to use the characteristics of good visual aids: bigger, simpler, easier to read. Because ideas flow in narrow columns across the page, you must use bullet points and trigger words. This prevents you from writing notes in complete sentences that are less useful during a speech, when there is no time to stop and read them.

The third advantage to horizontal notes is their flexibility. A motion to a judge with three issues is organized in three columns. If the judge interrupts and asks to hear about the third issue first, the brain can easily adjust. Like a map, horizontal notes can be read in either direction—left to right or right to left.

Imagine an argument regarding liability that addresses duty, breach of that duty, and resulting damages. This illustration shows only the topics in the following examples, leaving out all the detailed bullets:

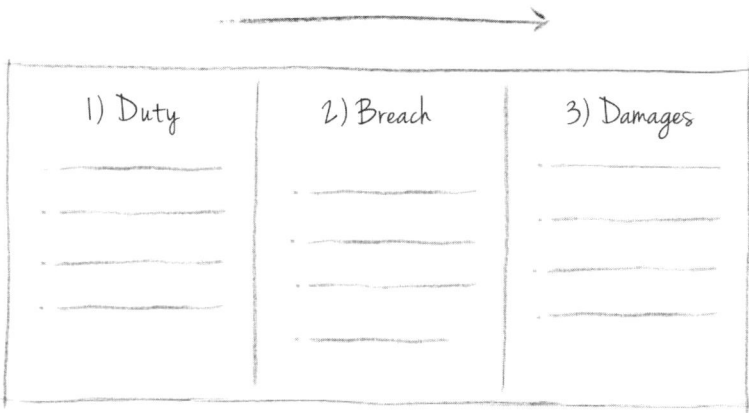

You first address the issue of duty, next describe how that duty was breached, and finally discuss damages. Your brain tracks along with the horizontal notes, your hands gesture along the shelf using the gentle double karate *chop*, and the listener thinks, "I see what you're talking about."

The ways you think, gesture, and make notes all share the same horizontal pattern. And, when you suddenly can't remember your next thought, you know exactly where to look.

If there is one problem with horizontal notes, it has to do with the listener's perspective. When your gestures track your own notes from left to right, your ideas appear backwards to your listener, like this:

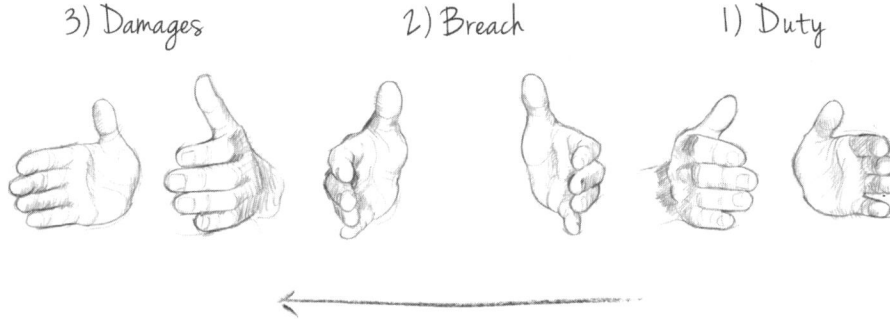

Here is the obvious solution: reverse your horizontal notes and let your gestures follow from right to left. A judge, jury, or arbitrator will see them flow from left to right.

Consider an argument regarding a company's financial losses for the first quarter. Your notes would look like this:

Your gestures follow your notes across the page:

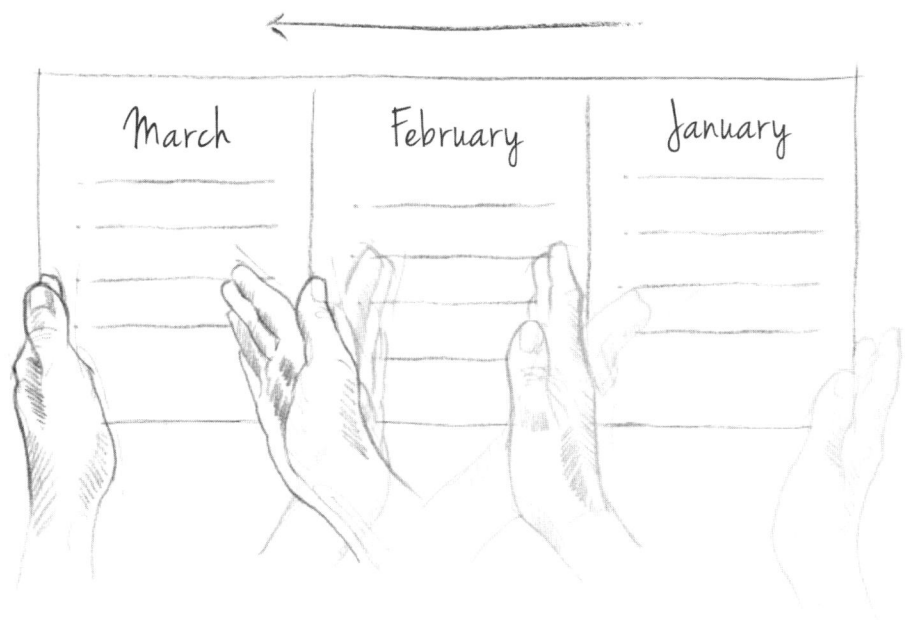

Your listeners see this:

With some practice, this idea becomes second nature. You are doing it for your audience. Simply remember: all patterns start to your right.

1. Practice using your notes. Stand up and talk out loud while using your notes. Speaking with notes is a skill that must be practiced. There is nothing particularly natural about glancing at notes while speaking and making regular eye contact. Work on it.

2. Read when you need to. If you need to look carefully at your notes to orient yourself, simply say, "Let's move on." That generic transition line justifies returning to your notes to see what's next in the structure. When you look at the notes, take your time. Listeners know what you are doing, and they aren't bothered by it. They're thinking about what you just said, or the question and answer they heard during examination. Jurors don't mind interruptions. Looking at your notes offers them a kind of break, resembling a commercial on TV or radio ("We'll be right back after this short break …"). Once you finish looking at your notes, return to looking your listeners in their eyes and speaking directly to them. If you do, they'll be patient when you consult your notes.

When you look, *really* look at your notes and read what is written there. Glance backward at the topic you just covered. If you forgot to mention something, fix the problem by saying, "Excuse me, I neglected to mention something important about that last topic." In this way, you turn the lemon of forgetting into the lemonade of "something important." Listeners will pay close attention when you tell them it's important. No harm is done. One reason advocates are so glued to their notes is that they are petrified at the prospect of forgetting something important. You needn't be afraid of forgetting. Give yourself time to look over your notes and make sure you have covered everything important in the previous topic before moving on to the next.

Plan to Forget

Many advocates bury their noses in their notes because they're gripped by the fear, "What if I forget?" But that's the wrong question! The proper question to ask and answer is, "*When* I forget, how will I recover?" That you will forget periodically while speaking under pressure is a given. Think how easily you can lose your train of thought when conversing with friends. You pause and confess, "I lost my train of thought. What was I talking about?" If this happens regularly during casual conversation, it's bound to happen during formal presentations. The obvious solution? Plan to forget. Know that it is going to happen, and be prepared for when it does.

As we have suggested, the transitional utterance "Let's move on" can be a useful way to explain and justify your taking a look at your notes and pausing to gather your thoughts. You are moving on, so it makes sense to refer to your notes to see what is next. Or, you can use the same line simply to stop and think. Fact finders will understand what you are doing. You have announced that you are moving on, and they see that you are thinking. At this moment, trust silence and be comfortable with it. Trust that they are watching your cognitive wheels turn. Take your time and think about what should come next.

If you are between topics and cannot remember your next area of discussion, simply say aloud the question that is in the forefront of your mind: "What's next?" Having asked that question, look at your notes and find the answer. This is a common storytelling device, especially when telling a story to children:

> Then Goldilocks knocked on the door. What happened next, boys and girls? The door swung slowly open.

You can use this same device in your opening statement when narrating what happened:

> Then they signed the contract on October 28th. What happened next? On November 3rd, the plaintiff...

But what if you can't remember a precise fact, such as a date or dollar amount? One way to deal with that problem is to say:

> Now the date the contract was signed (*you suddenly can't remember, so you say*)...

I want to get this exactly right (*and consult your notes*) ...

the date was October 28th.

As you say, "I want to get this exactly right," look purposefully at your notes and check the fact to get it right. This behavior is an indication of due diligence; it can even boost your credibility.

The final plan to offset *forgetting*, which may win you some sympathy, is to simply say what you say in conversation: "Excuse me, I lost my train of thought." If it doesn't appear to bother you, it won't bother your listeners. After all, it's natural, and it happens periodically to them in conversation.

Before you try any of these techniques, pause long enough in silence to make sure you really can't remember what you wished to say. The next thought may not quite be on the tip of your tongue, but it is almost certainly somewhere in your brain. Give yourself a moment to find it. Be aware that it is at such moments that the time warp is most oppressive. Don't panic. Take your time. See if the thought is somewhere in your head. Take a breath, open your hands, and give yourself a moment of silence. If the thought doesn't materialize, act on your plan to forget and use one of the techniques suggested above. If you practice saying these "plan to forget" lines before you need them, you will be ready to use them when the moment comes. Say them aloud right now to begin that process:

Let's move on.

What's next?

What happened next?

I want to get this exactly right.

Excuse me, but I've lost my train of thought.

Scripting as a Preliminary Step

Some advocates find it absolutely essential to write out their presentations before creating the final version of their notes. If writing feels like a necessary part of your preparation, don't fight it. But recognize that writing is only an interim step in the process. You do not write in the same style in which you speak—in law school you were trained to write like a lawyer, not conversationally. No one really speaks in the language used in legal writings. Even if you had a perfect photographic memory and could stand confidently and recite accurately every word you had written, it wouldn't sound natural. A stilted style loaded with legalese is not very effective when spoken aloud; it sounds too literary and artificial. However, if writing out your speech helps you organize your thoughts, do it. But then create a visual aid you can easily read, or make horizontal notes. Once you've got a structure on paper, practice improvising with that structure.

Avoid Thinking Backward

It cannot be emphasized strongly enough that you should *not* try to recite in order to replicate, word for word, what you wrote. If you attempt this, you will find yourself "thinking backward." Your brain cannot simultaneously think backward to what you wrote and forward to what you are trying to say. Your thought process will grind to a halt. Your script is merely one version of your presentation—and probably not the best version. When you say it aloud the first time, you will use the same structure but different words to convey it. When you practice it again, yet another set of words will emerge to embody that same structure. Think forward. Describe your ideas with newly minted sentences that will be different each time. The structure remains the same, even as the exact words change. Every time you practice, you will improve by sounding more spontaneous and more persuasive. To understand how thinking forward can help keep your train of thought on track, consider a concept from cognitive psychology: chunking.

Chunking

The human brain prefers to receive information in chunks. If a substantial amount must be recalled, the brain likes to aggregate those many bits of information into chunks so that there are fewer things to remember. Your ten-digit phone number is a good example of this. Because ten numbers are hard to remember, your phone number is "chunked" into three parts: (555) 123-4567. The parentheses and the hyphen visually group those ten numbers into three chunks that will be easier to remember.

Conversely, the brain also prefers for large, complex concepts to be broken up into smaller, more manageable chunks, such as:

1. personal information
2. educational background
3. work experience
4. day of the accident

Your notes show the important topics (or chunks) that you will talk about as an advocate. One way to help your listeners follow your structure is to indicate clearly when a topic or chunk is ending or beginning. Chunking can refer to the macro-level structure of big topics and concepts, but it is also a useful concept for understanding the micro-level of sentence structure. Techniques in the next chapter, Your Voice, will build upon this structure.

Structure: Primacy and Recency

Communication theories refer to *primacy* and *recency*, meaning that listeners pay close attention to the beginnings and endings of presentations. Minds often wander in the middle, as attention and retention drop. When listeners get a signal that the end is near ("In conclusion …"), attention increases again.

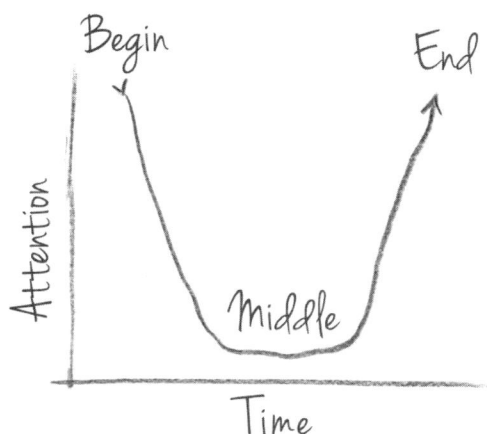

You have a small window of opportunity to capture their interest. If you seize it at the beginning, it's easier to hold it. You must be stylistically and substantively compelling right from the start. If you sound as if you don't care about what you're saying, or you stumble over your words, you squander this opportunity. Don't begin with meaningless filler such as:

> This is a simple case ... (*unlikely or you would have settled*)
> I've just got a couple questions ... (*never true*)
> How are you today, Mr. Wong? (*you don't really care*)
> Members of the jury, opposing counsel just told you a lot of facts ... (*a pointless observation*)

Whenever possible, say something at the beginning that you want the listener to remember, such as: "Isn't it true that you were texting at the moment your SUV struck Ms. Hennessey?" What juror isn't going to pay attention to what follows that question? Granted, it is not always possible to start with such an obvious "grabber," but you have to *sound* immediately engaged and be interested yourself. Always begin with an energy and enthusiasm that suggests you are taking the listener somewhere intriguing. When you can't capture their attention substantively, you can always grab and hold it with the style of your delivery.

As the words themselves imply, to *grab* and to *hold* attention takes energy—vocal and physical energy. As an advocate, you must work hard immediately. Don't slouch on the lectern or put your hands in your pockets to start. You cannot afford to warm up slowly and gradually become dynamic, enthusiastic, and interesting several minutes later. If you do that, by the time you've warmed up and achieved a certain level of skill, the listener's mind will have wandered off.

Even if you begin in a way that immediately captivates the listeners, it is important to recognize that no one listens attentively 100 percent of the time. Minds wander. Attention fades in and out; as a result, retention rises and falls. Knowing this, you as an advocate have the goal of regularly recapturing those wandering, inattentive minds and inviting them to pay attention once again.

Since beginnings and endings are good, create more of them. Rather than conceive your presentation as having only one beginning and one ending, clearly delineate each topic area. Begin each new topic with a headline (primacy) and explicitly mark the conclusion of the topic (recency). If topic A of your direct examination is your witness's *educational background,* announce that topic before you begin the line of questions—"Ms. Bittova, let's focus on your educational background"—marking the moment of primacy. Before moving on to topic B, *professional experience,* close out topic A: "We've discussed your educational background, so now let's talk about your professional experience." A cross examiner might headline this way: "We've discussed who was responsible for maintaining the furnace; now let's talk about the required annual inspections." In an opening or closing in a criminal case, a prosecutor creates endings and beginnings by saying, "Members of the jury, I described the charges the state must prove; now let's examine the evidence that proves those charges." When topic areas are demarcated in this fashion, your presentation will have many beginnings and endings. Each time a new topic is headlined and closed out, the daydreaming listener is invited to pay attention once again. Attention may still dip in the middle, but not as much.

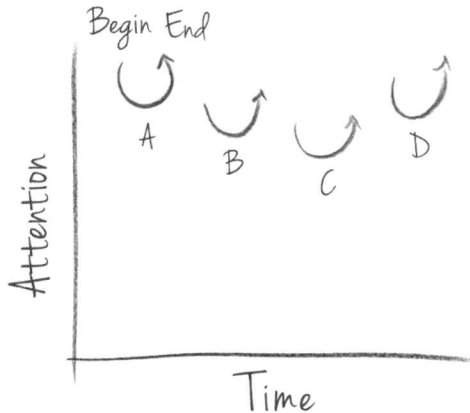

Exploiting the laws of primacy and recency will help you remember the structure of your presentation. Once you have stated aloud to the fact finder the topic area you are discussing, you will discover it is easier to focus your own thoughts, as well as your jurors', on that one subject. It will assist your memory if you practice saying aloud just the headlines that begin and end topic areas. Once you can make connections between these areas, then you'll have the structure clear in your mind. When judges, juries, or arbitrators can follow your structure, it is easier for them to pay attention.

Attitude is a Tactical Choice

Your attitude is apparent in your demeanor and tone of voice. In everyday life, your attitude adjusts to fit each situation. You adopt a different attitude while offering a toast at a wedding than if delivering a eulogy at a funeral. A job interview demands a different attitude than a family gathering. Your attitudes change without your consciously thinking about it. As an advocate, however, you need to contemplate and choose the attitude that best fits your goals. If you don't, your attitude may be out of sync with your words or your tactics. You may appear unfeeling and insincere at one extreme, or emotionally out of control at the other.

For an opening statement, select the most appropriate attitude for your theme. Choosing the right words is not enough. To be credible, you must sound as if you mean what you say. Your feeling has to fit your words. For example, an opening statement may begin with the emotional theme, "This is a case about a tragedy." But delivered without a suitable attitude, the sentence is devoid of feeling. With a flat tone of voice, lacking sincerity, the advocate might as well have said, "This is a case about broccoli." Say not just the words, but express the feeling implicit in those words.

Pick and practice your attitude for direct examination. Why not be friendly when examining your own witnesses? If you want the jury to like them and find them credible, talk to them as if you like them and find them credible. Unless there is good reason not to, speak to your witnesses on direct with the socially engaging energy you use when talking to your friends and colleagues. Be yourself in conversation. Occasionally you may have a strategic reason to put some emotional distance between yourself and your witness, but that happens rarely. Much of the time your attitude can be polite and curious. Because you already know the answers, it is important that you adopt an attitude that makes you sound genuinely interested in what your witness has to say. You want the judge or jury to be curious about the answers, so ask the questions with an attitude that is:

curious
friendly
interested
agreeable
surprised
probing
puzzled
intrigued
understanding
compassionate
sensitive
sympathetic

Cross examination presents a different attitude challenge. The best practitioners caution against cross that is relentlessly hostile and aggressive. "Cross doesn't need to be *cross*," as the saying goes. If you begin with questions to which the witness must agree, it makes sense—tactically—to sound agreeable. If the witness fights with you on those questions, he is the one who appears hostile and inappropriate. Good trial lawyers describe how it is important to "let the jury get there first." By that they mean, get tough only after the jury expects or wants you to do so. If it happens, consider shifting to these attitudes:

frustrated
annoyed
skeptical
amazed
astounded
shocked
incredulous
baffled
sarcastic
contemptuous

But be careful. Once you go negative, it is easy to become trapped by these hostile attitudes and never change. It is tiresome and annoying to watch a cross that is unrelentingly peevish and snotty. Control your emotions. Shift them to keep the witness off-balance on cross. Change to a new attitude as you change to a new line of questions. If the witness becomes increasingly hostile in response to your aggressiveness, switch to a different attitude. Suddenly be neutral or even polite so the witness cannot anticipate your next move. If voices have been raised in a shouting match, suddenly ask a question more softly to regain emotional control and the moral high ground.

Your attitude can also be a powerful tactical weapon in closing argument. You want to appeal to both hearts and minds. Some of those arguments may be more emotional to appeal to feelings and emotions. Other arguments may be coolly rational and logical.

For every phase of the proceeding, pick the attitude that fits what you are saying and the goal you wish to achieve.

Mirror Neurons

A recent discovery of how certain neurons fire in the human brain reveals how important it is—neurologically—to immediately control your body's actions when speaking in public. This revelation begins with a true story about a monkey and a peanut.

The setting is a neuroscience lab in Parma, Italy. A monkey is being used to study a part of the brain that controls movement. His motor cortex is wired in such a way that when he reaches to pick up a peanut, the action generates a specific sound—*bzzzzzzzz*—through a computer in the lab.

While on a break, his brain still wired, the monkey is sitting in his cage, completely still. A researcher walks into the lab, notices peanuts near the cage, and reaches to take one. As he does so, the monkey's brain responds—*bzzzzzzzz*—and the computer makes its characteristic "reaching" noise. The monkey doesn't move a muscle, yet the neurons in his motor cortex mirror the action of the person he is watching, triggering the signal as if he had moved.

The researchers are astounded! This incident reveals what are now called "mirror neurons." They exist in the brains of monkeys and humans. One could sum up the discovery of mirror neurons with this rhyme: *Seeing is being, and viewing is doing.*

Our brains mirror other people's actions as we watch them, as if we are performing the action ourselves. Mirror neurons are one reason why human beings are so intuitive about others. We are not just seeing them; we are being them, neurologically. These neurons help explain why watching sports is so compelling, and why fans become emotionally swept up in the action. An athlete's impossible catch or improbable leap is engaging because the fan is not just viewing the action, she is doing it, mirroring an amazing play in her brain. *Viewing is doing.*

This also explains why people cry at sad movies. Accomplished actors trigger our mirror neurons with the "real" emotions we see on their faces and in their bodies, then our mirror neurons communicate with our brains' limbic, or emotional, systems. When we watch a well-acted scene in a movie or a play, the actors have connected their actions to our feelings. We have the experience we see.

Similarly, you can exploit the mirror system to inspire feelings of confidence and comfort in yourself and the people watching you. As you stand before a panel or jury, your brain is firing in certain patterns that control your actions. If you could take a simultaneous functional MRI of your brain and those of your listeners, their brains would be mirroring the patterns in yours. Seeing you is like being you. Viewing what you are doing is the same as doing it themselves.

If you act like a nervous person—doing the dance of discomfort with your feet; gesturing with small, fast, and jerky motions; letting your eyes dart around the room—your brain fires neurons in nervous patterns. Those same patterns fire in your listeners' mirror neurons, and it makes them uneasy.

If you behave comfortably, you make your audience comfortable. Establish immediate control of yourself and influence how listeners feel about you. Stand still, breathe mindfully, gesture expansively, and make eye contact. Those actions will calm you down and project confidence and comfort. Your fact finders will mirror those feelings back at you. That is when you connect genuinely with your jury, making advocacy an exciting and inspiring challenge that you enjoy.

Using Electronic Evidence in the Courtroom

The use of projected electronic evidence in the courtroom is increasingly popular, encouraged by judges who understand its efficiency and power. While it is beyond the scope of this book to delve into how to select and design effective slides, the dynamic interplay between advocate and projected image is an important aspect of courtroom communication.

Once you have selected the appropriate images to project, the next challenge involves timing and focus. How long will each image remain on the screen so that the jury has time to read, absorb, and comprehend it? During that time, where do you direct their focus to achieve that goal?

It is instructive to compare these questions of timing and focus to what you do in a professional conversation. If you hand a document to a colleague and say, "Read this," her perplexed response will be, "The whole thing? Which part? Where?" Instead, you tell her where you want her to focus, "Read that last paragraph, especially the final sentence." Then, most importantly, you stop talking to allow her to do that. If you don't, your colleague will glance up quizzically and complain, "So quit talking! Let me read!" This is precisely the dilemma that jurors confront with electronic evidence. Are you asking them to read the whole thing? Which part? Where do you want the focus to be? Once they know what to read, stop talking so they can do it.

Inside the courtroom and out, the ubiquity of PowerPoint has led speakers of all stripes to believe—erroneously—that human beings listen and read simultaneously. Nothing could be further from the truth. They can't! Your colleague cannot do it in conversation, and neither can your jury in the courtroom.

The challenge of pausing to read is exacerbated by how much the effect of adrenaline's time warp makes silence seem to last too long. When you stop talking in the courtroom, silence appears to creep—along—very—slowly—so you leap in and talk too soon. Time's up! Or so it seems. Long before the viewer has had time to read and comprehend what's on the screen, you move on. The jury misses the point. The most compelling slides will not have the persuasive impact you desire if you don't stop talking long enough for that to happen.

Practice these basic elements of delivery when advocating with electronic evidence on a screen:

1. Identify what is on the screen, for the record. Before you may project the image of an exhibit on the screen—or "publish it to the jury," in the arcane language of advocacy—it must first be identified, marked, authenticated, offered, and accepted into evidence. After you have identified the document and had it marked and the witness has authenticated it and provided any other evidentiary foundation, then you offer it into evidence. Once the witness testifies that the document is, for example, the admitting record from the hospital emergency room, and you have authenticated it as a business record, you offer it into evidence. "Your honor, I offer plaintiff's exhibit 18 into evidence."

Once the exhibit has been accepted into evidence, you ask the judge, "May I publish it to the jury, your honor?" With the judge's permission, you may project the image on the screen. To create a record, you must then identify it as marked. "This is plaintiff's exhibit 18, the admitting record from the hospital emergency room." Even if an exhibit has been pre-admitted, you can't generically refer to a slide saying, "This is the admitting record from the hospital emergency room." For the record, be specific and use the exhibit number.

2. Tell the jury what they are looking at. During opening statement, if (and only if) you are using electronic evidence pre-admitted and approved for use in opening, be explicit in telling the jury what they are looking at. "Members of the jury, this is exhibit 18, the hospital emergency room admitting record dated July 27th of last year." Tell them where to look so they can confirm what you are saying: "If you look at the top of the document in the center, you can see the name of the hospital. The date and time of the admission is to the left." Stop talking and give them time to find, focus, and read. Take a breath and count silently to yourself, "One Mississippi, two Mississippi, three Mississippi," to wait three full seconds.

If the exhibit you are projecting is a letter, then explain it—saying, for instance, "You can see the defendant's letterhead at the top of this document, and the date it was written is below that to the right. Below that on the left are the name and address of the person who received it." Don't assume everyone in the jury sees what you see. You may be talking about the date at the top, while a juror is fascinated with the swirling signature at the bottom.

During closing argument you might say, "Let's look at the evidence. When the emergency room doctor testified, you saw plaintiff's exhibit 18. On the screen is the admitting record from the emergency room dated July 27th of last year. Let's look at it together."

3. Tell them precisely where you want them to look. Be specific. Don't assume that the jury knows where to look without your guidance. "Look halfway down the page, find the word 'Diagnosis,' and read the ER doctor's handwriting next to it."

4. Communicate with your computer operator politely. If you are fortunate enough to have an assistant operating the computer, talk to the assistant and be polite and respectful as you do so. Your jury will most likely identify with that person more than with you, so how you talk to that colleague is important as to how they perceive you. "Richard, please zoom in and magnify the middle of that document for us." Be explicit, and be prepared to talk through the inevitable technical glitches that will arise when using technology.

5. Explain your pull-outs and highlighting. Unlike attorneys, many jurors do not work in a setting where they are regularly subjected to PowerPoint presentations. Tell them what you are doing when you pull out and magnify a portion of a document or highlight text in yellow. What is self-evident to you may not be to them. "With that entire document in the background, we're going to zoom in and magnify the middle of that page. Please highlight that paragraph in yellow so the jury can read it easily." Keep their attention by explaining what is happening on the screen.

6. Allow time to read and absorb the text. If you show them a longer portion of a contract, letter, or e-mail, make sure that they have time to read it, which is only the beginning of the challenge, and have time to fully comprehend its meaning, which is your point. Let it sink in for a moment.

To insure comprehension and understanding, consider letting the jury read the text to themselves silently before you do so out loud. Tell them where to look, what you want them to read, and give them plenty of time to do so. Then, you read it aloud. Introduce the sentences you want them to focus on by saying something like, "Defendant's exhibit number 26 is the contract in dispute in this case. I want you to read the paragraph at the bottom of page 3. Richard, please zoom in on that paragraph and make it bigger. Please take a moment to read that, members of the jury." Then stop talking. This is the most obvious, yet most difficult, thing to do. Stop. Pause longer than you think is necessary. Your familiarity with the document means that you already know what it means, so you are ready to move on. But your jury, which is not accustomed to reading legal contract language, may require much longer than you do to read and comprehend.

7. Read out loud the deeper meaning you intend to convey, not just the words. As was discussed earlier in the section on how to read aloud, speak the text in phrases with heightened emphasis to clarify your meaning. If your expressiveness feels a bit over the top, it's probably exactly right.

8. Don't project your outline for opening or closing. Outlines are boring, and they are not visual aids. Despite that, we hear advocates say, "I just put the outline of my opening on PowerPoint to help me remember it." Even if an outline on the screen helps you remember, it doesn't qualify as something that will visually aid the jury's understanding. Even if it benefits you, it should not bore them.

Consider carefully which words you choose to project. Slides do not always help. Sometimes a powerful theme for opening statement or closing argument is neutralized when flattened out on a two-dimensional screen. "Desperate men do desperate things" may be more compelling when delivered with a matching tone of desperation in your voice. Even a simple theme in a contract case, "A *deal* is a *deal*, members of the jury," is likely more self-evident when delivered with an expressive, matter-of-fact, don't-you-agree tone—"A deal is a deal!"— than when it is blandly read off the screen. Say what you mean, and mean what you say.

9. Turn the slide off periodically. When the screen goes blank, the focus of the jury returns to you. A common problem while speaking with projections, and belittled as "PowerPoint poisoning", is the overdose of images that never stop. "One damn slide after another" is how visual communication guru Edward R. Tufte both sums it up and puts it down. (Read his short monograph *The Cognitive Style of PowerPoint* to understand fully his critique.)

Make the screen go blank, then talk to the jury with their full attention on you. When you turn it back on and show another image, that change will capture their attention and help to keep them interested. Don't leave an image on the screen long after you have moved on to another topic. Get rid of it immediately. Lingering slides are a distraction. Likewise, don't project an image long before the jury knows what it is. They will be confused, trying to figure it out, and stop listening to you as they do so. Save slides for the right moment. Timing is critical.

10. Practice timing your slides. Ask someone completely unfamiliar with your case, and preferably not a lawyer, to observe as you practice with your slides. Ask this viewer to give you specific feedback about how long it takes to read and comprehend each slide. Simple images may require very little extra time, but complicated text with many words may require a surprising length of time to be read and fully absorbed. Once you project an image on the screen, tell the viewer where to look; then ask that person to raise his hand when he completely understands the point of the slide. Don't just guess—solicit specific feedback about the timing. Try this with several viewers if possible. Know how long it takes for others to read and absorb your complicated slides.

Finally, in addition to understanding clearly the rules of evidence, consult the books by experts regarding visual communication to inform your selection of images. Edward R. Tufte has written several helpful and beautiful books about visual communication. Author and trial advocacy teacher extraordinaire Frank R. Rothschild has co-authored books about using electronic evidence. As with everything about courtroom advocacy, make sure you know what the judge for your trial will allow and what technology is available in her courtroom.

Summary

To think and speak under pressure, you must understand and ultimately exploit the time warp, a phenomenon created by adrenaline that makes time appear to slow down. When you experience this, be aware of it and don't speak too quickly. Embrace your altered perception and make silence a conscious part of your technique. To get into the zone of concentration, listen to the silence before you speak, then integrate that silence into your presentation, pausing briefly between phrases and sentences. This gives your listeners a few moments to think about what you just said. Persuasion happens in the silence, so use it to give judges, juries, or arbitrators time for their echo memory to process your words.

Don't read or recite from memory; get comfortable with structured improvisation. Create notes that help structure your presentation and can serve as a visual aid. Write big, legibly, simply. Practice using your notes. Plan to forget; it's going to happen.

If you need to write out your speeches or examinations as a preliminary step, do! Then reduce your structure to a simple outline or bullet points. Don't try to think backward to what you wrote; think forward to what you're trying to say next.

Focus on creating more primacy and recency in your presentations; use clearly delineated beginnings and endings as topic areas. Think and speak in phrases or chunks. Silence is punctuation made audible.

Choose an appropriate attitude for each phase of your proceeding. If your attitude is clear, you help fact finders understand exactly what outcome you advocate.

Plan your visuals, especially electronic demonstrative aids and evidence, so they are clear and precise. Limit the number of slides you show, and don't make them dense with text. Then, practice with them. Resist leaving this to chance!

Talk to Yourself

"Hear the silence first, then use it to think while speaking."

"Give them time to echo, so it sinks in."

"Stand back from the lectern to see the notes easily."

"Adrenaline makes time slow down, and gives me time to think."

"Plan to forget, and recover."

"Think forward to what's next, not backward to what I wrote."

"Pick an attitude."

"Help my fact finders understand my visual aids."

Chapter Three
Your Voice

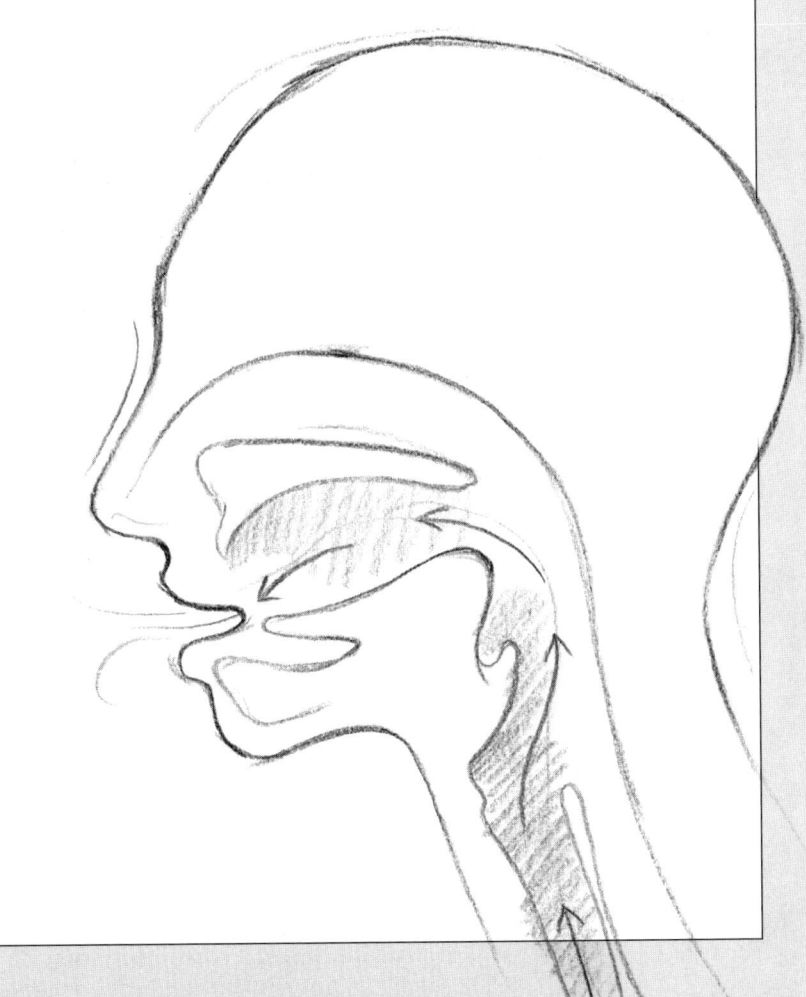

In everyday conversation, how do you use your voice expressively? How do you adjust your pace, volume, energy, pitch, and tone when talking to different people about various topics?

To speak more persuasively as an advocate, begin by listening to your own voice in daily conversation. You may not be aware of it, but in order to communicate better, we all continually make adjustments in our speech. Previously we explored the issue "What do I do with my hands in conversation?" Now ask similar questions about your voice: "What do I do with my voice when talking with friends and colleagues? How does my voice change to be expressive and appropriate in different situations?" You certainly pay attention to *what* you say in conversation; now pay closer attention to *how* you say it.

Listening to Yourself

Your goal as an articulate advocate is to push beyond what you do naturally with your voice. You need a technique that will give you the vocal power and stamina to speak persuasively and audibly for extended periods of time. If you are soft-spoken, you must get comfortable speaking at a consistently greater volume. If you are shy and introverted, you must learn how to transcend those tendencies and become a zealous advocate for your client's cause. If you talk very fast, you must be able to slow down and control your pace. Most important, you should be reliably fluent and articulate every time the judge looks at you and says, "Counsel, you may proceed."

If you think your voice is shrill or squeaky, you can help the intonation drop slightly lower by breathing more efficiently. We address breathing in this chapter. Be aware that you cannot make radical changes in the pitch of your voice. You can, however, support your own sound better, and that will make your natural voice sound more authoritative. Likewise, if your voice cracks or sounds scratchy, better breath support will help.

Another challenge is to evaluate your own voice objectively during recorded playback. When you hear your voice, you probably sound rather odd—to yourself. It's important that you get past this hypercritical, subjective response, as it's unlikely that you sound funny or peculiar to anyone else.

Improving your voice begins with an honest assessment of its current state. To evaluate your voice accurately, it helps to understand why it sounds funny to you on a recording. The answer involves two different ways we hear ourselves speak. When your vocal cords vibrate, those vibrations travel both through the air (to a listener's eardrums or to your own) and through your body. You can observe this phenomenon by gently putting your index fingers in both ears and reading these next sentences out loud. Your fingers block the vibrations that normally travel through the air to reach your eardrums. What you hear instead are additional vibrations traveling through the flesh and bone of your neck and skull to your inner ears. Now remove your fingers from your ears, and place the palm of one hand on your upper chest right below your neck. Read this sentence aloud, and notice that as you speak your upper torso also vibrates, which you can feel in your upper chest. This feels particularly intense because your body itself is vibrating, not just the air near your ears.

Without these lower-pitched vibrations conducted by flesh and bone, our own voices often sound "nasal" to us. However, there's nothing wrong with your voice! Begin to use it with greater power, confidence, expressivity, and authority. Abandon your self-critical response and tackle the real challenge: using your voice more persuasively.

Your Lungs and Diaphragm

Chapter One discussed the necessity and mechanics of breathing consciously. This not only calms you down, it also allows more oxygen to reach your brain and enables you to speak with greater power, projection, and control. The muscles that govern respiration include the diaphragm and the intercostal muscles between your ribs. All of these should be warmed up before you begin speaking as an advocate.

Observe your breathing as you read this paragraph:

Your autonomic nervous system controls your breath. A small, subtle movement is taking place in your lower torso. Now begin to breathe consciously, and inhale more deeply. Did you notice how much more completely and efficiently you breathed when you fully inflated your lungs? Take an even longer, deeper breath. Work the muscles of respiration more vigorously; push against your belt.

Intercostal Muscles and Your Rib Cage

The ability to consciously control your breath is the foundation of mastering your voice. In addition to the diaphragm, the intercostal muscles between your ribs help the lungs expand. Place your hands on the bottom of your rib cage, at the sides of your body about halfway between your waist and armpits. Take a deep breath, and feel the outward movement of the intercostal muscles as your lungs expand. Breathing consciously and deeply creates a three-dimensional expansion: your abdomen moves forward, your ribs push out at the sides, and your back extends to the rear.

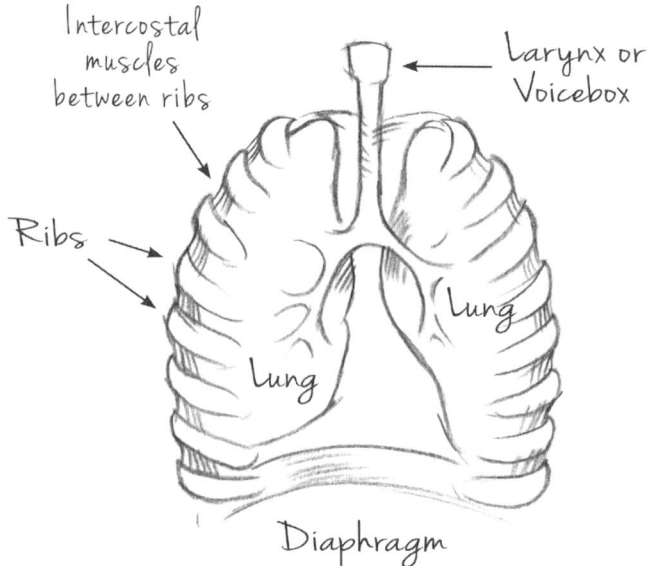

It is important to discern two types of deep breathing. The first is the slow, relaxing breath described in Chapter One. This is the conscious breathing you do to calm down prior to speaking. As you sit at counsel table, warm up the muscles of respiration slowly, gently, and carefully. Use deliberate, deep breathing to calm your emotions as well as to prepare to channel the imminent adrenaline buzz. When a judge asks you a question during a motion or appellate argument, breathe deeply as you listen to the question. During direct examination, you have time to breathe when a witness is providing an extended answer, when you pause to look at your notes, when you walk with purpose in silence to a new location, or when you simply stop to think. During opening, closing, or cross, there isn't time for these slow, measured inhalations; they simply take too long. You will use more vigorous breathing, requiring more energy to adequately support and project your voice.

Project Your Voice with Breath

Recall from Chapter One the advice to breathe in and speak out. Take a breath, and on exhalation, speak. Don't misunderstand—this doesn't mean that you should inhale, exhale, and then try to speak. That cannot work, since your lungs would be empty when you needed to speak. Breathe in to fill your lungs, and once they're filled, use the air in your lungs to power your voice.

From the dawn of time until the advent of the microphone, public speakers had to be able to project their voices at great volume. Imagine Caesar addressing the Roman legions, or Lincoln delivering the Gettysburg Address to twenty thousand listeners—outdoors and without amplification!

When William Jennings Bryan spoke at the Boulder, Colorado, Chautauqua in 1900, the local paper reported that his booming voice could be heard a mile away on the University of Colorado campus (the roar was heard, though exact words were not discernible). In the past, orators had breath control techniques that enabled them to project their voices loudly and for long periods of time.

Today there remain some stage performers with extraordinary breath control and volume. Classical singers and stage actors are still trained to be loud enough to project to the last row of the balcony. Opera singers, in particular, are the Olympians of music-making—the sheer strength of the compressed air in their lungs allows them to be heard over an entire symphony orchestra, without amplification. The stereotype of fat opera singers does have a kernel of truth, in fact. That extra weight becomes ballast for the remarkable breath support necessary to produce loud, ringing high notes. When they take in a deep, abdominal breath, their extra body weight helps the abdominal wall drop forward, flattening the diaphragm and pulling a large volume of air into the lungs. This air is then compressed by the power of the working abdominals, diaphragm, and intercostals, which push it back up and through the larynx, where the vocal cords vibrate. The length of vocal cords determines voice type and range. Whether a resonant *basso profundo* or a high tenor, a mellow alto or a dynamic soprano, all big voices are powered by muscle and practice.

This type of muscular breathing has direct applications for advocates. You may need to fill a large space with your unamplified voice and be heard by the judge, a witness, and the hard-of-hearing members of the jury. Only consistent breath control makes every word audible. On cross examination, for example, the important word is usually at the end of the question: "Captain McCarthy, you did not call for help for three hours?" It is natural for your voice to trail off at the end as you run short of breath and your voice drops to a lower pitch. But you can't leave the jury wondering how long it took Captain McCarthy to call for help. This is important, or you wouldn't be asking the question. To be loud enough, do what singers and actors do: use your abdominal and rib cage muscles to stay loud—or get louder—as the question comes to an end.

Vocal Fatigue

Speaking at length as an advocate sometimes causes vocal fatigue. It's important to understand that the solution for a tired voice lies not in your larynx, but in your abdomen. Your voice tires from a lack of breath support. If there is not enough air passing over your vocal cords, you will add stress and tension to your throat as you attempt to project. This makes you sound worn out and eventually hoarse. If you feel your voice getting tired, focus on your breath support. Work the abdominal muscles more vigorously as you inhale.

Breathe mindfully when pausing briefly between topics. Pause longer between sentences to breathe deeper. Breathing from the belly will save your voice.

Your Larynx and Vocal Cords

Your diaphragm pushes air out of your lungs so that it flows up your trachea, or windpipe, to your larynx. The larynx is the "voice box" in which your vocal cords are housed. Though sometimes pictured as two thick rubber bands stretched across your larynx, the vocal cords really aren't cords. They are two folds of cartilage attached to the sides of your larynx with a space between them. When you speak, air passes through the folds, causing them to vibrate. The greater the amount of air passing across your vocal cords, the greater the volume, or decibel level, of your voice. A very soft whisper uses so little air that the cords don't vibrate, while a full-throated shout causes them to vibrate vigorously.

Manipulating your larynx will not increase the volume of your voice. If you add unnecessary tension to your neck, throat, and vocal cords, you will only limit your volume (and possibly damage your vocal cords). Keep your neck and throat relaxed so that air can pass across your vocal cords unimpeded by excess tension. The more open, relaxed, and properly aligned your neck and larynx, the more freely, easily, and vigorously your vocal cords can vibrate.

Once your neck and larynx are aligned and your diaphragm and lungs are working properly, your voice will have all its natural overtones and will sound its best. Do not try to drop your voice lower, except occasionally for emphasis. Trying to speak lower, to make your voice something it isn't, may well damage your vocal cords.

It's difficult to gain technical control over the vocal cords, since you can't look directly at them. You must rely on physical sensation. Some voice teachers compare the feeling of an open throat to the sensation felt when inhaling quickly and deeply in a gasp of amazement. With your fingers placed gently on your larynx, take in a vigorous inhalation of surprise. Feel how the larynx moves downward as the throat opens. That is the feeling you seek—a relaxed, open throat.

Articulators and Articulation

The articulators—your jaw, lips, and tongue (which interacts with your teeth and the roof of your mouth)—transform a column of vibrating air into intelligible words. Furthermore, your face has forty-four different muscles, a large number of which are involved in clearly enunciating each word, and articulating your ideas. The more energetically and precisely you work these muscles, the more easily the listener can understand you.

In conversational speech, articulators are often underused, and many syllables and consonants—especially final consonants—are dropped in conversation. Although we write:

Q: When are you going?
A: I'm going to leave about nine.

We often say this, using fewer syllables and dropped consonants:

Q: When ya goin'?
A: I'm gon' leave 'bout nine.

In conversation, the context and melodic contour of a sentence helps people understand each other. Lack of articulation generally isn't a problem. To be understood as an advocate, however, you must give each consonant its proper enunciation. Taste every consonant. Savor them, even those you may drop in conversation.

Warm Up to Be Articulate

The best way to achieve the clearest speech is to enunciate vigorously, paying attention to the small details of pronunciation. Elocution once was taught in grade schools, but now it seems quaint. The word evokes visions of an overly formal style, taught by an uptight pedagogue with a starched collar and ramrod straight posture. Actors, singers, and broadcasters still study diction, but for the rest of us, the study of declamation and delivery has pretty much gone out of style.

Nevertheless, speaking clearly in order to be understood requires precision. Think of your articulators as an important component of your technique. Warm them up before you speak, just as an athlete warms up before a competition. Prepare them to go to work immediately, and you are much less likely to trip over your own tongue at the start of your presentation. (Fluency errors early in a presentation have two downsides: they undermine your confidence and can make a negative first impression.)

Here are a number of ways to warm up. Find a private place and a couple of minutes to stretch and invigorate your articulators and the muscles in your face. If you are now in a private place, stretch the muscles of your face to learn this technique.

Open your mouth as wide as possible; simultaneously, open your eyes and lift your eyebrows. (Don't be shy, no one is watching.) Stick out your tongue as well. Continue this stretching action by compressing the same muscles. Withdraw your tongue, and scrunch up your face by pursing your lips and squeezing your eyes closed. Now alternate between these two different actions. Stretch and then squeeze, stretch and then squeeze your facial muscles several times. Next, try to move all your facial muscles to the right side of your face, then to the left side. Lift all the facial muscles up, then down. Move your face around at random, stretching every muscle. Now stop, and feel the warm, subtle sensation of increased blood flow in those muscles. Warm up to be articulate right from the start.

Next, warm up the lips and the tip of the tongue. Repeat these nonsense syllables over and over, increasing the speed as you get more comfortable and warmed up:

niminy piminy, niminy piminy, niminy piminy (etc.)

To form the consonant "n," place the tip of your tongue behind your upper front teeth; the "m" and the "p" are formed by the lips. Take a deep breath and exaggerate as you articulate this pattern again. Work the articulators crisply and vigorously, more than you ultimately will use them while speaking. This will prepare you to speak clearly and easily.

Say the same pattern again, this time moving the pitch of your voice from the lower register to the upper register. Move the pitch up and down to warm up your vocal cords as you warm up your articulators.

The next exercise works the articulators from front to back. Say:

butta gutta, butta gutta, butta gutta (etc.)

Say aloud the consonant "b" and feel how it is formed on the lips. "T" is formed with the tongue and teeth. The "guh" sound is formed in the back of your mouth when the back of your tongue arches up to meet the roof of your mouth. Repeat the exercise and feel the shifting of the consonants from your lips to the back of your mouth. Exaggerate and say it again, moving the pitch of your voice from lower to higher to lower to higher.

You also can warm up your articulators by using tongue twisters:

Girl gargoyle, guy gargoyle

Swiss wristwatches

Yet another way to warm up the articulators is to begin a mental list of words that trip your tongue. Collect those words and use them as a warm-up exercise. When you trip over words with consonants that you find personally challenging—perhaps repeated "s" sounds in the phrase "statistically significant"—use that word or phrase as a warm-up:

> statistically significant, statistically significant, statistically significant (etc.)

Say it a number of times, exaggerating the articulation and gradually increasing your speed.

Overarticulate these warm-up exercises to increase the blood flow into the muscles of your face and to prepare to speak. Of course, you will not exaggerate your articulation as you speak in court, but it is the best way to warm up.

With the muscles of respiration and articulation warmed up and ready to work, the next step is to make choices about how you will channel the energy these muscles provide. To make these choices, you first need to give yourself time to do so, which leads us to a discussion of controlling the pace at which you speak.

Making Persuasive Choices

Speaking persuasively requires that you make verbal choices spontaneously. As you select the words to say, you must simultaneously decide which words to emphasize in order to make your meaning clear. In a motion or argument, which sentence deserves extra emphasis? In a series of questions, which ones merit particular stress? Within each question, which words are most important? Much as you use a yellow highlighter on the printed page, you can use your voice to audibly highlight important words, clauses, and sentences. But it takes time to make these choices. Recall from Chapter Two that adrenaline slows time for you. Use that time—and the silent moments it provides— not only to think about what you are saying, but also how to say it expressively.

Silence is the secret ingredient of persuasive speech. If you are uncomfortable with silence, you will talk too fast; you won't take time to think about what you are saying, and your sentences will be poorly constructed and awkwardly delivered. You will trip over your tongue.

You will speak first and think second, as your lips move and words emerge before your brain has decided what to say. Also, talking too fast often leads to an excessive use of thinking noises—*uh* and *um* and *okay*—as the brain struggles to find more time to think. Eventually your self-confidence collapses, and your train of thought threatens to crash and burn. Speaking persuasively, on the other hand, begins with controlling the pace at which you talk—and to do so, you must be comfortable with silence. (Recall from Chapter Two that if listeners don't have time to think about what you are saying, they won't remember it, much less be persuaded by it.)

Energy Up, Pace Down

Persuasive speech requires more energy than casual conversation. That is why being natural is not enough to get the job done, and why merely being comfortable as an advocate is not synonymous with being convincing. One source of the necessary energy for persuasive speech is your own adrenaline. It provides the body with extra energy to cope with potentially life-threatening situations. When people are anxious, they often refer to "coping with lots of nervous energy." Co-opt that feeling, and focus on the energy already available within you. Say to yourself, "Good! I'm nervous. That will provide me with extra energy—and energy is the raw material of communicating persuasively."

When you think of a speaker with lots of energy, you may suppose that energy and speed are synonymous: an energetic talker is a fast talker. Not necessarily. Energy can be used to speak quickly, but it can also be used to speak emphatically. When advocates speak persuasively, they use lots of energy—for emphasis and clarity, not speed. When people speak persuasively, they often become more energetic while simultaneously slowing their pace. The increase in energy signals the importance of what is being said, and the slower pace gives the listener time to think about, and be persuaded by, what is being said. The energy goes up and the pace goes down.

By warming up and using your breath and articulators, you raise your energy. To slow the pace, employ the concept of chunking. The brain functions best when it has time to formulate language in chunks; likewise, your listeners understand better when they receive your message in small bits.

Speak in Phrases, Not Whole Sentences

In everyday conversation, you gather your thoughts into sentences constructed one chunk at a time. Words grouped into a phrase are a chunk; phrases are arranged into bigger chunks, or sentences. On the written page, punctuation—commas, periods, question marks, exclamation points, dashes—signals a chunk's conclusion. Sentences composed around one idea are grouped into paragraphs, and larger paragraph chunks are delineated visually by indentation and added spacing. When you speak, you provide audible punctuation to your listeners.

At the very beginning of a presentation, when you most likely are feeling the time warp created by adrenaline, you should consciously speak in phrases and use small gaps of silence between them to think. The silence between phrases and sentences signals to listeners when the chunks begin and end. If there is no silence, there is no audible punctuation. Confusion ensues. Imagine the visual (and cognitive) challenge to a reader if this paragraph were printed as follows, without any visual punctuation:

> at the very beginning of a presentation when you most likely are feeling the time warp created by adrenaline you should consciously speak in phrases and use small gaps of silence between them to think the silence between phrases and sentences signals to listeners when the chunks begin and end if there is no silence there is no audible punctuation confusion ensues imagine the visual and cognitive challenge to a reader if this paragraph were printed as follows without any visual punctuation

All the words are correct, but without proper punctuation, it is much harder for the reader to parse and comprehend. Spoken language presents a similar challenge. Listeners need signals—audible punctuation—to mark where chunks start and stop. Whether these chunks are phrases, sentences, or paragraphs, their meaning becomes unambiguously clear through intermittent moments of silence.

Because of the adrenalized time warp, you don't have an accurate sense of what a slow or fast pace really is. Rely on speaking in phrases to give your brain sufficient time to construct each sentence or question carefully, one chunk at a time—sometimes a single word becomes a cognitive chunk. As we discussed in Chapter Two, the brain likes to think in chunks, a strategy that fits perfectly with the listener's cognitive processing. This is not the same as speaking slowly in such a way that your creeping pace becomes annoying. Speaking slowly might suggest that you should move your articulators slowly, but that would sound ridiculous. (You ... do ... not ... think ... or ... speak ... one ... word ... at ... a ... time.) *Speak in phrases, not whole sentences* is a more practical instruction for the brain to follow.

If you are a really fast talker with a rapid-fire delivery, control the pace by regularly taking your finger off the metaphorical trigger. Speak in phrases, and in the silence between them, allow the fact finders to digest and be persuaded by what you have said. Although the words may fly out of your mouth, you still can give the listener time to process those verbal bursts.

Practice saying important sentences and questions at a slower pace to provide contrast. If you say everything at the same quick pace, then it all sounds the same and appears to be of equal importance—and that is never true. To mark their significance, important utterances should be spoken at a slower, more deliberate pace.

The Mechanics of Phrasing

Imagine the encounter when a parent, unhappy that a teenager has stayed out too late, attempts to persuade the errant teen not to do that again. The pace slows down; the energy level goes up. Speaking a phrase at a time and maintaining the energy level, the parent says emphatically:

If you *ever*
come home *again*
that late,
you
will be *grounded*
for a *month*.
Are you *listening?*

Say that out loud, persuasively! Say it deliberately, one phrase at a time, and say it like you mean it. Say it like you heard it said to you, or like you yourself have said it.

Use your pace to signal the significance of the message; find a deliberate, speak-in-phrases rhythm that affords abundant time for it to sink in. Do not speak quickly. If this warning were delivered at a fast pace it would not sound as credible, nor be as convincing. In persuasive speech, energy is used to emphasize key words; the pace remains slow and deliberate.

We speak in phrases whenever we recite text together as a group. For instance, citizens of the United States are speaking in phrases when they recite the Pledge of Allegiance:

I pledge allegiance
to the flag
of the United States of America,
and to the Republic
for which it stands,
one phrase
at a time ...

The Pledge is a perfect, and familiar, example of speaking in phrases. Use it to set the proper pace at the beginning of every presentation.

First, decide what you want to say, and then practice saying it with a deliberate pace modeled on the Pledge of Allegiance's rhythm. Using that rhythm, tell yourself:

That's the rhythm
I can use
to control the pace that I'm speaking.

There are many well-known examples of orators speaking in phrases. In his inaugural address, President John F. Kennedy challenged the nation with these words, delivered persuasively, one phrase at a time:

Ask not
what your country
can do for you;
ask what you
can do for your country.

If you recite that quotation aloud but say it quickly, it loses its power. When you say it slowly, and emphasize the key words, you begin to sense the power of speaking a phrase at a time. Say Kennedy's words aloud again, more slowly than before. Hear the short gaps of silence between the phrases. Stretch them even longer. The slower you speak, the more important the idea appears to be.

Vary the Pace

As an advocate, you will not say everything a phrase at a time, slowly and deliberately. Speak in phrases when what you are saying is important—when you want the listener to think carefully about what you are saying. As we discussed in Chapter Two, beginnings and endings of presentations should be carefully crafted to take advantage of the benefits of primacy and recency. Between these beginnings and endings, speak in phrases whenever you say something particularly noteworthy, whether emphasizing facts in an opening or arguments in a closing, or asking key questions during examinations. You can talk faster when covering preliminary information. A transitional sentence such as, "Moving on to what happened on July 15 ..." would be a logical place to speak more quickly. A listener doesn't need to hear that transitional sentence a phrase at a time, nor the preliminary information that follows. You will make choices continually about how and when to vary your pace to fit your persuasive purpose.

Be flexible enough in your pacing to slow down and speak in phrases whenever you come to more crucial points. When you arrive at this information, state it a phrase at a time, slow the pace, and keep the energy high. This gives your listeners time to think about, remember, and be persuaded by what you are saying.

The necessary variation in pace—slow to fast to slow to fast—is analogous to the movement of a train pulling out of the station. Start speaking slowly to get your train of thought on track. That deliberate pace will signal significance, when listeners are paying close attention at the beginning. Inevitably you will speed up as you get going, like a train building a head of steam. Slow down again at each station—each important point along the way—to make certain your listeners are on board.

Since your brain composes sentences a phrase at a time, you are, in a sense, always speaking in phrases. When something is important, the gaps between those phrases become slightly elongated; there is more time, and hence more silence, between them. When you speak more briskly about preliminary or transitional matters, you still speak in phrases, but the gaps between the phrases grow shorter or disappear altogether.

Use Your First Utterances to Set the Pace

Each time you speak, the first words out of your mouth set the pace for what follows. Be careful, therefore, about rushing through your first few sentences:

> May it please the court. This is a case of mistaken identity. Joshua Franklin was in another state on the night of the robbery.

Whether stating your theme or using common boilerplate, advocates usually begin speaking very quickly. Boilerplate is rote information and not as interesting as what follows. When your first utterance is too fast, that hasty tempo tends to persist, and it will prove hard to slow down when the more substantive sentences are reached.

To avoid this problem, practice the first sentence aloud. Consciously set a slower, more deliberate opening pace. Say it a phrase at a time, rather than tossing it off quickly. Say it with real meaning, rather than as a meaningless ritual. Legal writing expert Bryan Garner argues that "May it please the court" is not a question to be delivered with a rising, questioning inflection. He believes it is a statement, deserving the emphatic descending inflection from a Stars Wars movie: "May The Force be with you." Say it aloud, authoritatively, and feel the difference.

Begin Sentences Deliberately

Once you are past boilerplate and have launched into substance, continue to control the pace. The advantage of speaking more deliberately, one phrase at a time, is that the slower pace, and the additional thinking time between phrases that it affords, gives you greater cognitive control. You have more time to consider what you are saying while you say it. If you begin by adopting a delivery punctuated with short, frequent gaps between phrases and sentences, then when one of those gaps is slightly prolonged, it's hardly noticeable. The silences become a kind of insurance against the derailing of your train of thought, enabling you to recover and move ahead. In conversation, you begin sentences without knowing how they will end. Use silence to think your way through long, complex sentences without ever stumbling or correcting a word.

Eliminate Thinking Noises

In conversational speech, many people frequently use the thinking noises *uh, um,* or *ah.* This is not an issue of intelligence or education; it is habit. Even highly educated speakers tend to use thinking noises far more often than they are aware. And awareness, or a lack thereof, is precisely the problem. Some speakers habitually use ten, fifteen, or even twenty *ums* per minute! Try counting the *ums* a mediocre speaker uses; you'll be surprised by what you hear.

Do you have an *um* habit? Like all habits, this one is subconscious and reflexive, so you may feel no compelling reason to stop—until you hear yourself on a recording. (Listen to a message you've left on voice mail.) It's no wonder that a problem so ingrained through daily repetition is difficult to control. If you know how often you say *um,* you'll be motivated to stop.

Thinking noises are an excellent example of why you can't simply tell yourself to be natural, when being natural may very well include the excessive, annoying *um, uh, like,* and *you know* of ordinary conversation. Once you're speaking as an advocate, it's too late to begin thinking about eliminating this persistent habit. You must work at changing it far in advance. Make it your goal to use no thinking noises at all—not in court, not in conference rooms, not on the phone, and not while talking to clients. Strive to be the always-articulate advocate.

Thinking noises typically occur when you speak in phrases but don't use silences as punctuation. In the place of silence, you insert a one-second, monosyllabic *um*. This noise indicates that you know it's your turn to speak but you need a second to think of what to say next. Lasting almost always about one second, and occurring on the same musical pitch in the speaker's voice, thinking noises lend a monotone quality to speech that is both distracting and annoying.

Certain words also can function as thinking noises. The expression *you know*, often inserted between phrases and sentences, gives the speaker an additional second to think. Children, teens, and even many adults use the word *like* in the same way. Nothing is *like* a clearer indication that *like* people haven't fully acknowledged *like* their professional status than this *like* annoying and childish verbal habit. Summer associates at law firms often are shocked to discover that speaking with this accent of adolescence is *like* highly undesirable. If you talk like a child, people don't take you seriously as a professional.

Another reason that thinking noises are *um* irritating is they intrude on the listener's thinking time. Just when your audience needs a second to consider what you have said, the thinking noise fills the silence like static on a cell phone connection. It interferes with the listener's cognitive processing. *Um* and *uh* are both irritating and counterproductive. Fortunately, they are also completely curable.

Mind the Gap

Passengers in the London Underground system hear an announcement over the public address system whenever a train pulls into the station: "Mind the gap. Mind the gap." A pleasant voice reminds passengers that there is a gap between the platform and the subway car. This phrase, "Mind the gap," is particularly helpful when trying to break the habit of thinking noises. Use it as a reminder to insert a gap of silence between phrases. Then follow the instruction: Mind the gap and pay attention! Do you have the urge to insert a thinking noise? Listen to the silent gap between phrases and sentences. It is a short pause, not a long rumination. During that brief moment, focus your mind on silence.

It is much easier to break a habit when you can give your brain a positive instruction, such as "Mind the gap," rather than a negative one: "Don't say *um!*" The negative instruction doesn't work because it keeps you focused on the problem, not the solution. Rather than tell yourself *not* to do something, encourage yourself to do something *better*. To break verbal habits, focus on the solution and mind the gap.

Remember, any thinking noise you are trying to eliminate is merely an audible indication that your brain needs a second to consider what you are about to say. You are verbalizing your need to stop—for one second—and think before speaking. The solution is to give your brain what it wants—a moment to think—but not to fill the needed silence with a bothersome and meaningless noise. Chapter Four, How to Practice, discusses in detail how to stop saying *um*.

Emphasis and Meaning

Speaking in phrases with plenty of silences helps you project your voice, speak clearly and precisely, compose coherent thoughts, and eliminate thinking noises. Adopting this deliberate pace is also an essential element of persuasion. Expressive, powerful speech takes extra time. If you talk too fast, there isn't much time to emphasize key words, which unlock the meaning of speech. Take the time to weigh word choice and expression. The accent you place on operative words can then be shaped to the maximum persuasive advantage.

Emphasis is vital for understanding speech. It is the *em*-pha-sis on the right *syl*-la-ble that makes words comprehensible. If someone speaks English with a heavy accent and places the em-*pha*-sis on the wrong syl-*lab*-le, it makes the listener's job more difficult. Intelligibility follows a progression: emphasizing the right syllable makes a word clear, and highlighting operative words makes a sentence understandable. Likewise, properly emphasizing an important sentence makes a paragraph of thought cohesive, and stressing your most prominent points makes your entire argument persuasive. During examinations, giving special attention to key questions clarifies your line of questioning. Emphasis gives spoken language a clear and persuasive meaning.

Imagine that, in a commercial dispute, you spoke the following sentence to a judge or jury: "She never promised the shipment would arrive by Tuesday." The meaning of that sentence will shift in subtle yet significant ways depending on which word you emphasize. Repeat this sentence aloud, emphasizing the key words printed in italics:

She never promised the shipment would arrive by Tuesday.
(maybe *he* did, but *she* didn't)

She *never* promised the shipment would arrive by Tuesday.
(with the stress on *never,* it is an absolute denial)

She never *promised* the shipment would arrive by Tuesday.
(you are waffling with the emphasis on this word)

She never promised the *shipment* would arrive by Tuesday.
(maybe she promised the invoice, but not the *shipment*)

She never promised the shipment *would* arrive by Tuesday.
(it could have arrived, but delivery wasn't guaranteed)

She never promised the shipment would *arrive* by Tuesday.
(it might ship on Tuesday, yes, but not arrive)

She never promised the shipment would arrive by *Tuesday*.
(maybe Wednesday, but not Tuesday)

And finally, one can also emphasize a number of different words in a single sentence:

She *never* promised the *shipment* would *arrive* by *Tuesday*.

This is what persuasive speech often sounds like.

An even subtler example of emphasis affecting meaning can be found in a famous quotation from Lincoln's Gettysburg Address:

government of the people, by the people, and for the people …

When we hear this line spoken, or speak it ourselves, it is usually delivered with the emphasis on the prepositions *of, by,* and *for*:

government *of* the people, *by* the people, and *for* the people …

What happens to the meaning if you shift the emphasis to other words? Filmmaker Ken Burns did just that when directing actor Sam Waterston delivering the Gettysburg Address in his documentary *The Civil War*. Burns believes that the proper emphasis is not on the prepositions but on the people:

government of the *people*, by the *people*, and for the *people* …

This shift in emphasis changes the meaning. The conspicuous repetition of the word "people" puts the emphasis, both literal and philosophical, in a different place. Say it aloud to get the feel of it.

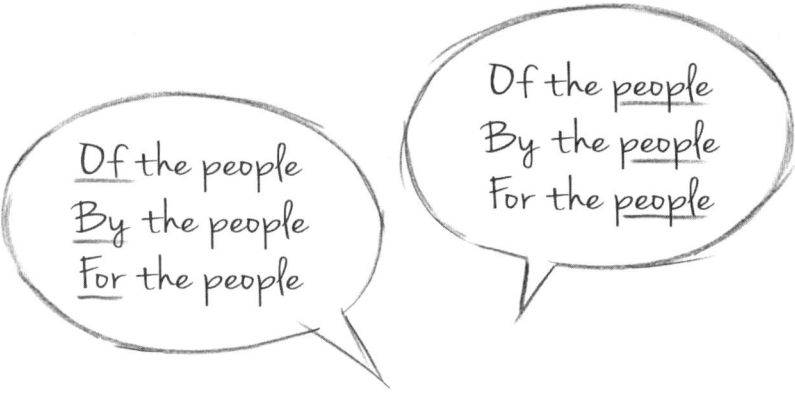

The art of acting rests largely on the power of emphasis to clarify and enrich meaning. The writer writes the words, and the actor speaks those lines as written. But the actor (together with the director) decides which words to emphasize. In *Death of a Salesman*, playwright Arthur Miller has Linda, wife of the salesman Willie Loman, say of her husband's desperate plight, "Attention must be paid." The playwright doesn't indicate which of those words should be emphasized; the actor must decide.

Attention must be paid.

Attention *must* be paid.

Attention must be *paid*.

Or perhaps every word in that short sentence is worthy of emphasis:

Attention ... must ... be ... paid.

Because acting is an art and not a science, all of these choices are possible. Using their trained voices, actors make such choices by the thousands, and these ultimately coalesce into an interpretation of a role.

Advocacy, too, is an art—one in which you must decide which words to highlight in order to convey your intended meaning. But the enormous difference between acting and advocating is that you do not recite from memory as actors do; you think on your feet. You make extemporaneous choices about emphasis. You do this all the time in conversation without a thought. Virtually every sentence you utter has at least one and often several words that you emphasize instinctively. Start listening to yourself and to others; hear emphasis, nuance, and expression in conversation.

Volume, Pitch, and Duration

Emphasis can be applied to words by varying volume, pitch, and duration. Often we stress the key words in a sentence by simply saying them louder. Say this phrase from the Gettysburg Address, speaking the italicized words louder:

government of the *people*, by the *people*, and for the *people* ...

Now say it aloud the traditional way, stressing the prepositions:

government *of* the people, *by* the people, and *for* the people ...

Try doing just the opposite with the volume of your voice. Stress the key words by saying them more softly (but still intensely) compared to the other words:

government *of* the people, *by* the people, and *for* the people ...

Emphasis also can be accomplished with pitch. Repeat our example using a higher pitch on the key words. This is the way we usually hear this famous quotation spoken. Now invert the intonation, using a lower pitch on the key words:

> government *of* the people, *by* the people, and *for* the people ...

Repeat these words yet again, using first a higher pitch and then a lower pitch to emphasize the italicized words:

> government of the *people*, by the *people*, and for the *people* ...

If you have trouble hearing your own voice navigate the subtleties of pitch variation, make an audio or video recording and listen to yourself.

Achieve emphasis with duration—by elongating the vowel of the accented syllable in the key word. Written language sometimes imitates this practice. Think of the different meanings of these words:

The repeated letter represents a prolonged vowel sound. Even in conversational speech, we often emphasize a word by slightly elongating accented vowel sounds. Listen to a recording of "I Have a Dream," Martin Luther King Jr.'s celebrated speech on civil rights. In it, he frequently emphasizes words by stretching their vowels:

> I have a *dream*, that one day this nation will *rise* up and *live* out the *true* meaning of its *creed*: "We hold these *truths* to be *self-evident*: that *all* men are created *equal.*"

Say this quotation aloud, slowly and deliberately. Speak it in phrases so that you have time to elongate the vowels of the words in italics. Then say it again, even slower, and stretch the vowels a bit more. Do you notice how the *pace* at which you speak is related to the *time* you have to be expressive with the words?

Likewise, draw out the vowels of key words in John F. Kennedy's inaugural address:

> Ask *not* what your *country* can do for *you*; ask what *you* can do for your *country*.

Say this quotation aloud, speaking it in phrases and emphasizing the key words—especially "you"—by prolonging their vowels.

You can, of course, read these excerpts in two very different ways. You can read the words blandly, with no attempt to capture their inspirational meaning. In such a rendition, every word is given roughly equal weight. Alternatively, you can focus on their meaning by emphasizing key words. Such an emphatic, expressive delivery will allow you to convey the meaning behind the words, and not merely the words themselves. Don't just speak the text; you must speak the *meaning* of those words. Proclaim it, with commitment.

Unlike the orators cited above, you won't write out your presentations in advance and then read them aloud. You will think on your feet, make choices about the words to use, and decide which ones need extra emphasis and intensity. Persuade your listener by varying the volume, pitch, and duration. You will be living, thinking, and speaking in the moment.

Why Not Just Read?

As we discussed in Chapter Two, unlike actors or broadcasters, very few advocates are trained in the art of reading aloud expressively. Unless you are experienced at reading aloud and have a well-developed, reliable technique for doing it convincingly, you won't be able to pull it off with any finesse. Why would you jeopardize your client's cause by relying on a specialized skill that you haven't cultivated?

Still, the urge to read in court is strong, and occasionally an experienced advocate will consider reading under certain circumstances. One seasoned litigator working on an emotionally wrenching case involving a truck accident worried the facts were so devastating that he might not be able to get through his opening unless he read it to the jury. Given these varied opinions, let's delve further into the question of reading.

We all read constantly. We spend our days reading, in fact. But reading silently is a very different skill from reading aloud persuasively. Indeed, all the hours that you've spent reading silently are a large part of the problem you face when attempting to read aloud. When you read silently, you tend to read very fast, and you'll probably read too fast when you read aloud. Most people do.

The faster you speak, the more likely you are to trip over your tongue and to read inexpressively. Key words won't receive the necessary emphasis; the music of your voice will sound stilted and flat, as though you're reading rather than talking—which you are! If reading aloud were easy, then virtually every literate person would be an effective actor or orator. Everyone would be able to pick up a script or speech and read it aloud with fluency and sincerity. But literacy and fluency are not equivalents. More to the point, even if you were a skilled reader, reading would be the wrong medium for persuasive advocacy.

When you read aloud, the music of your voice betrays that you are reading. Your range of means of expression narrows as you employ a more limited vocal range. Your voice falls into repetitive patterns that quickly become boring.

There is another pitfall for an advocate who chooses to read. Your writing style is different from your speaking style. Even if you took the necessary time to practice reading slowly and carefully, it would be difficult to sound convincing because of this stylistic difference. You neither speak the way you write nor write the way you speak. So even if you could read aloud effectively, your writing style (especially after law school has trained you to write like a lawyer) will sound stilted and overly formal when spoken aloud.

When delivering a motion or an appellate argument, you don't want to read because you will most likely be interrupted with questions from the bench. Shifting between reading a script and thinking on your feet while answering questions is a difficult transition. Don't read to the judge; talk to him instead.

But the best reason not to read is that it makes you less persuasive than when you are talking. Most likely you will stand at the lectern, stare at your notes, and periodically glance up furtively, in a way that no one mistakes for eye contact. You can't make sustained eye contact when you read. In a jury trial, you've got to look the jurors in the eye, and you simply can't do that if you are reading to them. You may need to look at them, tell them the kindergartner watched as his father took his last breath before the paramedics could help, and then ask for damages. To do that, you need a technique for talking, not reading.

When You Must Read

Although reading is rarely persuasive, there are times in court when you must read aloud: from a witness statement, for example, or from a deposition, expert's report, or written text projected onto a screen. When you're obliged to read aloud, read in phrases—slowly. Be aware that your brain, accustomed to reading silently and quickly, will be tempted to read too fast. Read deliberately, a phrase at a time, if you want listeners to fully comprehend the meaning of those words. Adopt a slow, deliberate pace and carefully emphasize key words to express yourself clearly. To achieve this goal, put slash marks in your text to indicate where to break the sentence into phrases, and underline the key words to emphasize.

> Ask <u>not</u> || what your <u>country</u> can do for <u>you</u>— || ask what <u>you</u> || can do for your <u>country</u>. ||

You now have an understanding of how to breathe, project your voice, and articulate your words. In addition, you can coordinate your brain and voice by speaking in phrases, minding the gap between phrases and sentences, and emphasizing key words with volume, pitch, and duration to make your meaning clear.

Now, back to gesture! What do you do with your hands to highlight persuasive speech?

Gestures and Emphasis

Your body not only powers and projects your voice with breath from the lungs, it also directs the expressivity of your voice through gestures. The instinct to gesture expressively is connected with the emphatic stress of key words in a sentence or question. As the gesture research of Dr. Jana Iverson has revealed, "gesturing and speaking are tightly connected in some very fundamental way in our brains."

Look for this connection in your own style. Watch a video of a presentation you have made, and look at your hands and listen to your voice. Place a sticky note on the television screen so that it hides your face from view, forcing you to focus on your gestures.

Observe that your hands instinctively know which words deserve emphasis. Even when your fingers or wrists reveal only the slightest impulse to gesture, those impulses occur on key words. These inclinations are not merely random fidgeting. Your hands know what to do. Trust them.

Gestures, as you'll recall from Chapter One, make you look and feel natural. But perhaps the foremost reason to liberate your instinct to gesture is to help your voice sound natural and expressive. Gesture makes your words and ideas clear and, ultimately, persuasive. Your hands know which words deserve emphasis and which vowels need to be stretched to achieve that. When you don't gesture, your verbal delivery suffers, and so do your listeners. While gesturing has a lot to do with how you look and feel as an advocate, it has an even larger role in how you sound. You could go so far as to say that listeners hear gestures—not the action of the gestures themselves, obviously, but the impact of those gestures on your speech pattern.

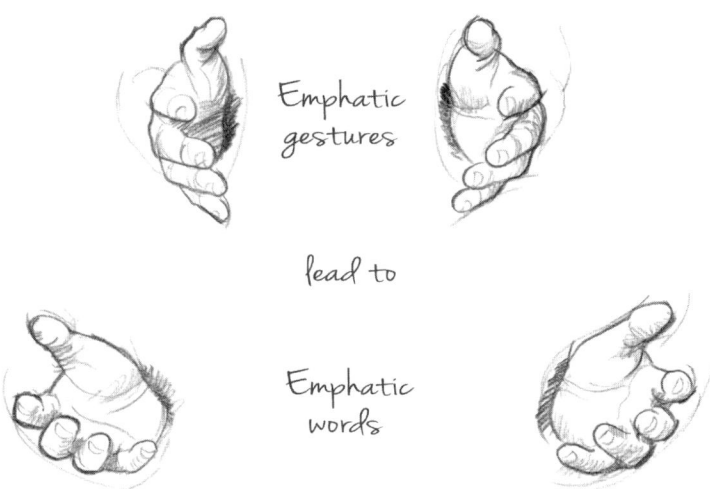

Monotone

The absence of gestures leads to an absence of emphasis on key words. Without emphasis on key words, the meaning of all words remains unclear—and you can't be persuasive if your meaning is not clear. Speech with no emphasis on key words slips easily into a difficult-to-listen-to, continuous stream of language stripped of the cues listeners need to grasp meaning. Monotone is literally monotonous, taking place all on one musical pitch.

Nobody—or more precisely *no body*—speaks in a monotone voice while gesturing. Such dull speech is always devoid of gestures. The next time you must endure a boring monotone speaker, transform your suffering into a learning experience. Ask yourself: Is she or he gesturing? Take your eyes off the speaker's face and focus on the hands. You will see that flat speech is linked to a lack of gesture. It follows that one good way to avoid monotony is to speak with your hands and use your gestures.

Conduct Yourself

The speed of your gestures has a direct impact on the pace of your speech. When your hands move quickly, you talk fast. If your hands move slowly and smoothly, your pace slows, too. As you speak, use gesture to shape the language in much the same way that an orchestra conductor shapes Mozart or Stravinsky. The speed with which the conductor moves her arms dictates the tempo at which the music is played. The connection between the speed of gesturing and the speed of talking is powerful: it is virtually impossible to gesture quickly while talking slowly. So if you want to slow the pace at which you speak, gesture more slowly and smoothly. Conduct yourself to control the pace.

Be Smooth

Smoothness characterizes the gestures and pace of a natural, comfortable speaker. Her movements are not fast and jerky; they are slow and smooth, and her pace of speaking is slower and smoother as a result.

This connection between the speed of gesturing and the pace of speaking is especially important at the very beginning of a presentation. It is important to start gesturing immediately, using movements that are slow, smooth, and expansive. If you do not, your inhibited and restrained initial gestural impulse will lead to small, fast, jerky mini-gestures, which will lead you to speak too quickly. Your train of thought will be more likely to derail, and you will make a weaker first impression.

If you begin gesturing at the outset, your natural movements will make you look and feel comfortable, and they will help you speak at a measured and deliberate pace. You will have more time to say carefully what you want to say. Hence you will look, sound, feel, think, and speak more effectively right from the beginning. The positive first impression you make will grab the listener's attention.

The secret of coordinating gestures and words at the proper pace is to practice this complex multitasking challenge alone, aloud, and on your feet. Don't leave beginnings to chance.

Practice Beginnings with Gestures

Decide, in advance, exactly what you are going to say at the beginning of your presentation. This is one of the few times that you should practice saying verbatim—word for word—what you want to say in the first few sentences. Do not trust that on the spur of the moment you will spontaneously say exactly the right thing. It won't happen.

Once you have found the precise wording of the very first sentences, then think about how to match your gestures to your words and ideas. This coordination, described in the discussion of jump-starting your gestures in Chapter One, involves deciding what words and ideas you will place on the shelf. Remember that this invisible, imaginary shelf is where you place your hands in the ready position prior to speaking. Plan logical gestures at the beginning.

You may decide that gesturing on the introductory boilerplate ("May it please the court, your honor, counsel, members of the jury ...")

doesn't feel quite right, although it is possible to gesture naturally even on the boilerplate. But immediately after that, what is the first substantive sentence you will say? In an opening statement it may be:

> This is a case about *broken promises*, promises made in a *written contract*.

Thinking logically, you have two subjects, *broken promises* and a *written contract*. As you say this sentence, place *broken promises* on the one hand, and *written contract* on the other. Try that, and see how it feels to put those two concepts on the shelf. Logically connect your gestures to what you are saying, so they function as a visual aid for the jury. Emphasizing key words lets your jury see what you're talking about: a broken promise, on the one hand, and a written contract, on the other.

> This is a case about *broken promises*, promises made in a *written contract*.

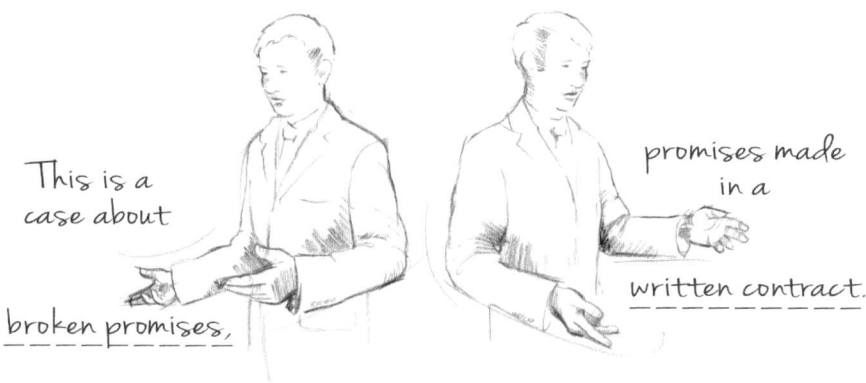

When you end your first substantive sentence with your body in this open and loose position, you make a positive first impression. The open position of the body says: "Trust me, I'm being open with you. I'm not hiding anything. I'm loose and natural, not anxious and stiff." In addition, you have jump-started your body's instinct to gesture, freeing your brain from any need to worry about what your hands are doing.

Plan and practice your initial gestures so that you can quit thinking about them. Instinct will take over when you gesture immediately.

Here is another example. Direct examination may begin with this instruction to your witness:

Please introduce yourself to the members of the jury.

Gesture toward the witness with one hand, as you say *yourself,* and toward *the jury* with the other.

A cross examination might begin with this question to an arson expert:

Mr. Tomkins, you *never* went to the *scene* of the fire, did you?

Gesture on the words *never* and *scene*.

Finally, closing argument often begins with a strong restatement of your persuasive theme. In a dispute between an inventor and the corporation that licensed his invention, the inventor's counsel might begin his closing argument by saying:

They *licensed* his inventions, made *millions* of dollars, and now they *refuse* to pay him the royalties he deserves.

This three-part theme could be placed on the shelf of gesture using three gestures in three different locations while emphasizing the words *licensed, millions,* and *refuse*:

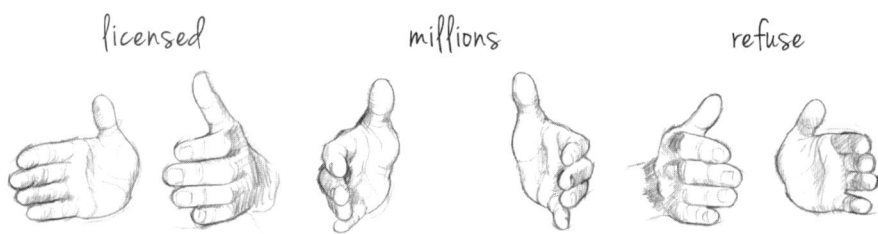

Once you've decided what you intend to say to begin, and which gesture will fit logically with those words, practice to get the feel of coordinating words with gestures. Thinking about your choice is not sufficient. Your muscles need to feel the action. Stand up in a room alone and speak aloud, practicing so that your gestures and your voice have muscle memory. (More about muscle memory in Chapter Four.)

There is one more thing you can do while sitting at counsel table to prepare your muscles to gesture immediately and naturally. This mental preparation for physical activity, *visualization,* is borrowed from professional sports.

Visualize Your Performance

Sports psychologists advise athletes to visualize their actions prior to competing. Athletes practice what they call "mental rehearsal." The Olympic skier imagines the moment when the buzzer sounds and she pushes off to plunge down the mountain in the giant slalom. The sprinter sees the moment when the starting gun goes off and he explodes out of the starting blocks. As an advocate, you can sit at counsel table and visualize the initial gestures you practiced. Visualizing an action that has been ingrained through practice frees you to gesture with even greater skill and confidence.

Athletes warm up and stay loose physically until right before a competition commences. Preparing to speak, you don't have that same luxury. You may have to sit at counsel table for a long time before you speak. Even if you warmed up earlier, sitting for a long time will cool you down again.

Visualization will help you to be ready when finally the judge says, "Counsel, you may proceed." As you sit there, think of the words you will say first. See in your mind's eye the gestures you'll use to accompany those words. Hear your pace of speaking in phrases in your mind's ear. Athletes use this visualization technique to win medals; you can use the same technique to win verdicts for your clients.

Prosody: The Music of Natural Conversation

Prosody is a general term for the musical elements of everyday speech. It encompasses tempo, rhythm, loudness, silence, and intonation.

These musical elements interact with syntax and meaning as you speak. We have examined some musical features already: emphasis on key words that lends a natural rhythmic cadence, loudness, and silence. This leaves intonation as the final element of prosody necessary for persuasive speech.

Intonation refers to the up-and-down movement of the musical pitch of your voice. This movement creates the subtle melody of natural speech. We have touched on the dreaded monotone, which lacks all melody or movement. Let's explore the desirable, persuasive alternative. No matter whether your voice is naturally pitched higher (soprano or tenor) or lower (alto or bass), you instinctively use a range of musical pitches as you speak, encompassing a lower, middle, and upper register. To speak persuasively, you need the technical ability to make periodic choices about the intonation and pitch of your voice.

Fortunately, much of the necessary variation of intonation or pitch results from simply emphasizing key words in a phrase or sentence. The very act of emphasis leads your voice to vary the pitch appropriately. That being the case, focus your attention now on the intonation or pitch direction of your voice at the end of a sentence or question. As your voice descends to a lower pitch or ascends to a higher one, you create "audible punctuation"—the "sound" of a period, question mark, or exclamation mark.

Audible Punctuation

Compare the movement of your voice's pitch at the end of a sentence to going up or down the steps of a staircase. When your voice descends to a lower pitch, it seems to walk down the steps. This is the audible period. When it ascends to a higher pitch, it walks up the steps, creating the sound of an exclamation mark. When you ask a question, the pitch slides upward, to a question mark.

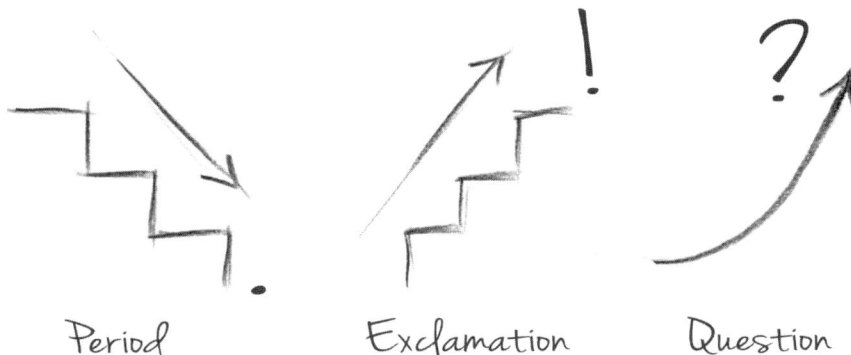

Say aloud these three utterances, using those three different patterns:

Use the audible period most often, just as you use periods most frequently when writing. When you descend to a lower pitch, don't force your voice into an uncomfortable or unnatural range. In a subtle yet significant way, walking down the steps at the end of a sentence conveys confidence and finality. If you expect to convince your listener that you know what you're talking about, you must sound like you believe what you are saying—and say it with confidence. This downward pattern helps to achieve that goal.

The other advantage to walking down the steps is that the finality suggested by the descending pitch buys you some extra time to think about what to say next. Both to your listeners' ears and to your own, that descending pattern signals a conclusion. The sentence is finished. Period. The silence that follows the audible period is like the white space that follows a written period. Your listener has a little extra time to think about what you just said. The sound of finality will help you mind the gap between sentences, because this intonation pattern makes your brain less inclined to fill in the gap with a thinking noise.

The audible exclamation mark, or walking up the steps, is useful when you need to add energy to your delivery. It comes in handy during the middle of your presentation if you sense your listeners' attention is lagging. Introduce your next topic and walk up the steps as you do so!

Use the audible question mark when you are asking a question, but be careful of using it when you are making a statement. The repetitive use of the questioning inflection, sliding upward at the end of phrases and declarative sentences, conveys a lack of certainty, confidence, and maturity. Listeners hear this upward inflection as "uptalk." If you wish to be taken seriously, expunge this vocal habit from your presentations as well as your professional conversational style. To avoid questioning yourself, walk down the steps.

Ending with Confidence

The law of primacy and recency tells us that listeners pay close attention to beginnings and endings. If endings are as important as beginnings, then you need a technique to signal reliably that you are finished. Whether saying the last sentence of a speech or the last question of an examination, walk down the steps to indicate that you are concluding. To reinforce the sense of finality, walk down the steps and slow down: go slower as you go lower. This powerfully conveys the message that you have finished.

You might end your opening statement with this plea:

> Members of the jury, at the end of this trial, we will ask you for a verdict in favor of
>   Acme
>   Industries.

Conclude a motion to a judge by saying:

> We ask the court to deny plaintiff's motion
>   to
>   compel.

Say that aloud and end the sentence by going slower as you go lower. Keep the volume up until the last word. Don't confuse lowering your pitch with lowering your volume. Walking down the steps is also the intonational pattern of the leading questions you will most often use on cross examination.

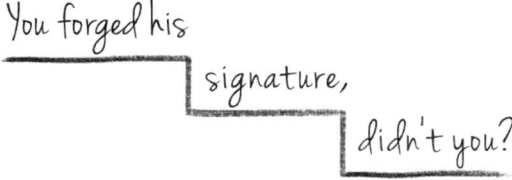

Tone of Voice and Attitude

Chapter Two discussed the need to pick an attitude. When you don't pick an attitude, you will default to the general attitude of "serious"—and serious, although appropriate to advocacy, quickly becomes boring and bland.

Once you choose an attitude, your tone of voice adjusts to fit it. Together, attitude and tone of voice constitute the underlying, driving energy of your vocal delivery. They go hand in hand, and both should be used consciously. If, for example, you choose to conduct a "soft cross" on a sympathetic older witness, you may choose "respectful of elders" as your attitude. Your tone would be deferential, measured, not too loud, and never impatient. Should the witness become difficult, however, you might change your tone to be firmer, respectfully at odds, or somewhat louder. Your attitude could stay the same by using phrases like "with all due respect, sir …"

Practicing Verbal Skills

Fortunately, you speak every day of your life, and this affords you abundant opportunities to practice regularly outside the pressurized environment of advocacy. For example, you can practice eliminating thinking noises during a casual conversation with a friend. That is the perfect time to focus some of your attention on eliminating *um* and *uh* as you mind the gap. Do you find yourself regularly stuck in traffic? What an opportunity to practice any of these elements of style (except gestures!). When you find yourself becalmed on the expressway, look at the clock on the dashboard and tell yourself to practice speaking without thinking noises for the next ten minutes. Then hold yourself to that obligation. Talk aloud for a full ten minutes and focus on eliminating thinking noises. When you hear yourself utter an *um* or *uh*, note that it happened, but don't stop and chastise yourself. Correct yourself and continue.

Brief, regular practice sessions are more valuable than less-frequent, longer periods of practice time. Since so much of the challenge of speaking effectively is getting started, the more often you practice, the better you'll become at the hard part: the beginning.

You can even practice these speaking skills on the phone. Put a sticky note on your phone that helps you eliminate thinking noises.

Summary

To use your advocate's voice persuasively requires that you learn how to listen to yourself objectively. Get over the notion that you sound funny; you don't.

The power of your voice comes from the muscles of respiration, including the diaphragm and intercostal muscles, working with the abdominal muscles. Clarity of articulation is achieved with the vigorous precision of the articulators: the lips, jaw, and tongue. When you work the muscles of respiration and articulation harder, your listener's job is easier.

Stressing the key words in your sentences and questions unlocks the meaning you intend. Emphasis is a function of volume, pitch, and duration.

The music of speech interacts with the meaning of your words. You can exploit this by walking down the steps to sound confident and conclusive. Use the audible period to eliminate the uptick of uncertainty.

Diligently practice the skills outlined in this chapter to savor the power and pleasure inherent in the art of advocacy.

Talk to Yourself

"Speak in phrases, not whole sentences. Break it into chunks."

"Between phrases, think in silence. It's not as long as it feels."

"Pause after the first phrase to set up a rhythm that works."

"Mind the gap between phrases to avoid thinking noises."

"At least one word in every phrase gets emphasized."

"Gesture immediately and emphasize key words with your hands."

"Avoid the uptick of uncertainty."

"Walk down the steps to end sentences decisively."

Chapter Four
How to Practice

Practice is the path to expertise. It is the only way to improve skill in any discipline. The more complex the skill, the more practice is required. Whether you want to be a better golfer, pianist, or advocate, solitary and mindful practice is absolutely essential.

You cannot acquire and improve any skill just by thinking, reading, or writing about it. Yet a surprising number of attorneys don't practice—alone and aloud—the skills of advocacy. Practice, while surprisingly hard work and challenging to fit into a busy lawyer's life, is also a creative act. Once you know how to practice efficiently and effectively, you will begin to enjoy it. For some people, practice isn't so much intimidating as it is silly. Others find it downright embarrassing. Yet if you want to be a better lawyer, you must overcome any resistance you feel and learn how to practice.

Practicing is a skill in and of itself—arguably the ultimate skill. If you know how to practice, you can improve any skill you set your mind—and body—to learning. This chapter will guide you step by step through the required skills, and you'll learn to practice smarter, with better results, in less time.

Some advocates want to believe that adequate preparation can occur somehow without practice as the final, culminating step. When asked how they prepared for an arbitration, trial, or advocacy training exercise, a surprising number of attorneys confess that they (1) read carefully through the material (silently); (2) thought about it; (3) wrote copious notes on a legal pad; and (4) prayed that all their reading, thinking, and writing would somehow coalesce into articulate, persuasive speech, on the first attempt, under pressure. Don't put your trust in this self-delusion.

Practice solo, at least at the beginning. Practicing alone, away from the critical eyes and ears of peers, colleagues, or spouses, provides an opportunity to make mistakes in private. It is nearly impossible to say anything well on the first attempt. Everyone needs multiple tries to express ideas well. Solitary practice gives you a chance to rough draft out loud, get ideas flowing, take risks, and make errors when nobody is watching.

Practice must be out loud. The muscles engaged in the motor skill of talking need exercise, just as those involved with breathing and speaking require warming up, blood flow, and conditioning through repetition. Practice that simulates the way you will speak during the legal proceeding should be your goal. Your entire body needs to practice standing still while talking and gesturing in the courtroom. For arbitration, practice advocating while sitting down and keeping your energy up.

And you should practice a lot—as much as you can. Busy law students and even busier practicing attorneys can find ten- or twenty-minute blocks of time to rehearse. In addition to such individual practice sessions, stage mock trials with colleagues. All practice serves to improve performance.

You must practice alone, aloud, and—ideally—a lot, in order to move ideas that you have read, considered, and written about from inside your head (your neocortex) to the tip of your tongue (your articulators). Persuasive advocacy is a motor skill.

To Know vs. Know How

There is a critical gap between your brain's capacity to *know* something and your body's ability to *know how* to do it physically. Practice bridges that gap. What your brain knows and understands, your body must practice to execute well. Suppose you wish to become an expert downhill skier. You read the best book available on the techniques required. Assume, too, that you're blessed with a photographic memory and are able to remember every technique described in the book. By the time you've finished reading the book, your brain *knows* a great deal about skiing. But such *knowing* doesn't mean that your body possesses the *know-how* to tear down a black diamond run. You have to practice what you learned in your reading to develop the physical know-how necessary to swoosh down a mountain like the ski patrol at Telluride. Your body's muscles, controlled by your motor cortex, need to *get the feel* of the required actions.

This chapter will help you practice to develop advocacy know-how. It will help you get the feel of it. To see the results you're hoping for, you *must* practice—because it is your brain that has read this book, not your body. Your body hasn't a clue about the meaning of the words and ideas in this text. To get the feel of it, practice is the only answer.

Lawyers used to have more opportunities to develop the know-how of trial advocacy than they do today. In the past, when small cases more often went to trial, advocates could learn the skills of advocacy through experience in the courtroom. For many attorneys in the twenty-first century, opportunities for on-the-job training no longer exist. Unless you are a prosecutor or a public defender, it is difficult to develop basic trial skills through actual work in real courtrooms. Given the risks of taking a case to trial today, cases are often too important to be entrusted to beginners. If you lack frequent opportunities to refine and polish your trial skills in trials, you have all the more reason to practice those skills, so that you'll be ready when the opportunity to take a case to trial comes along.

The lack of trial opportunities has led to an increasing number of trial skills training programs for practicing attorneys as well as law students. Participants in such programs, especially busy practitioners, frequently complain that they haven't had enough time to completely digest and assimilate the facts in the case file. They're right. And practice—alone and aloud—is the only way to overcome this problem. When you live with a real case over time, you discuss the case with the client, witnesses, colleagues, opposing counsel, judges, in depositions, and so on. You have lots of real-life opportunities to say the facts aloud before presenting the case to a jury. In the training environment, that out-loud experience is missing. Although you have studied the case file silently, chances are that you have never said any of the facts out loud. Once you overcome any resistance to practicing alone, aloud, and a lot, you can jump-start your ability to remember the facts of your case and to speak them confidently, even if you've had little time to prepare.

Practice: Resistance and Avoidance

It's unfortunate that "practice makes perfect" promises an impossible expectation. Forget perfection! Your goal in practicing is not to make yourself perfect but to make yourself better. Perfection as an advocate is not only out of reach, it isn't even desirable. The jury doesn't want you to be perfect, they want you to be human, with all the forgivable foibles and imperfections that implies. Your humanity makes you credible.

Practicing with a Mirror

There is a belief that practicing in front of a mirror will help you improve. We find such practice is usually counterproductive, unless you are working on subtleties of attitude and facial demeanor.

The most important reason to practice is to shed your self-consciousness. Mirrors, however, exist precisely to make the viewer self-conscious. You look in a mirror to make your "self" conscious of your hair, clothing, or makeup.

Since your goal in advocacy is to be fully aware of your audience—to be able to speak without being overly self-conscious—the last thing you want to do is practice with tools and techniques designed to emphasize self-conscious behaviors. Practice talking aloud as if to other people, not to yourself in a mirror.

Occasionally, though, using a mirror can help, so here is our suggestion: tape a piece of paper on the mirror so that it obscures your face, but leaves the rest of your body visible. This painless self-decapitation will allow you to focus on your body—and especially on your gestures. As you practice aloud, notice if your gestures are too small, too fast, or too jerky. The mirror now provides immediate feedback without making you excessively self-conscious.

Rationalizations That Inhibit Practicing

"I'm not an actor!"

Some diffident people feel that practicing aloud is synonymous with artifice, pretending, and fakery. Uncomfortable with the self-awareness that practice requires, they worry that their personal integrity and authenticity may somehow be violated. Often they declare, "I'm not an actor! I just can't fake it."

If you are in this group, take a leap of faith. Practicing doesn't make you phony or insincere; it will help you find your natural and authentic self when the pressure is on. Once you practice a skill, it becomes second nature, and if you practice enough, it will feel, appear, and be natural.

"If this were a real case …"

In training programs, some advocates declare that they are simply "too real" to practice. This rationalization often begins with the phrase, "Now, if this were a real case …" The reality of the case and the trial would supposedly inspire these people to perform well. Yet when asked for some evidence of this theoretical effectiveness, they can't make good on their own predictions. One imagines such people betting their money on athletes who are "too real" to practice, waiting for the real game to prove their mettle.

"I don't want to be over-prepared."

This is another frequently heard rationalization for avoiding practice. What this usually means is that the advocate tried to practice for a short period of time, felt uncomfortable, and quit—and then rationalized quitting as a fear of being overprepared. With a skill as complex as litigation, the odds of your being overprepared are less than the odds of your being struck by lightning during your underprepared opening statement, in the midst of which you may wish, in fact, to be struck by lightning—to end your suffering.

"I feel so silly."

There is one very real emotional challenge regarding practicing. Talking aloud in a room alone is typically taken as a sign of madness! It makes everyone feel, initially, a bit silly, and that feeling may be compounded by the unwarranted fear that someone is listening just outside the door. Frankly, the only solution to this problem is to get over it. Would you rather feel silly in private or in public? Would you rather feel a bit silly—temporarily—talking aloud in a room alone, or feel infinitely more foolish struggling in front of clients and peers in real life?

Since the case ultimately is your client's case and not yours, how do you suppose your client would answer if you were to ask: "Should I practice or not?" If you yourself were ever a party in a lawsuit, which kind of lawyer would you prefer: the one who is unable or unwilling to practice because she feels silly, or the one who comes into court fully prepared to fight for your cause?

Be Patient

Given how complicated these skills are, be gentle and generous with yourself as you practice. Be patient. Your progress will be gradual. The progression of steps in skill acquisition range from beginner to novice, to competent, then proficient, and, finally, expert. If you are a beginner, it will take you time, experience, and diligent practice to develop the skills to become a novice, then competent, and, finally, proficient. To become expert is an arduous process, but one well worth pursuing.

Novice → Competent → Proficient → Expert

Where are your advocacy skills on the skills acquisition continuum?

How to Practice, Step-by-Step

When you practice speaking aloud, your goal is to use, develop, and refine the cognitive skill of structured improvisation. Remember: you are not practicing the skill of reading aloud a text you have previously written; you are not practicing the recitation of words you have memorized; you will not practice in order to memorize your presentation word for word so that you can eventually recite it from memory. You will practice extemporaneous speech. You will practice giving your brain an opportunity to process thoughts into words in much the same way you do in everyday conversation, but with one enormous difference: you must be able to think and speak for much longer periods of time, strategically structuring your ideas while obeying the many rules of procedure governing what you can say and how you can say it.

Practice in order to repeat the same structure, but not the same words each time. Within the given structure, improvise your words, and vary them slightly. Your brain is fluent at this; now trust that you can do it for longer periods of time.

Before you talk, create horizontal or bullet point notes that detail the structure of your presentation. (Review Chapter Two for suggestions about creating the most effective notes.) Practice using them.

If you can, practice in the actual courtroom or conference room. If you can't, set up your practice room to simulate that reality. If you're practicing an opening statement or closing argument, specify an area across the room where the imaginary listener is seated. For a jury trial, place two chairs far apart enough to indicate the right and left ends of the jury box. Practice speaking to the imaginary jurors. When you practice an examination, place an empty chair across the room to mark the location of the witness. Your eyes need a target to focus on, so treat the chair as if a witness were seated there. Focusing your eyes will help focus your brain.

Run Your Body's Checklist

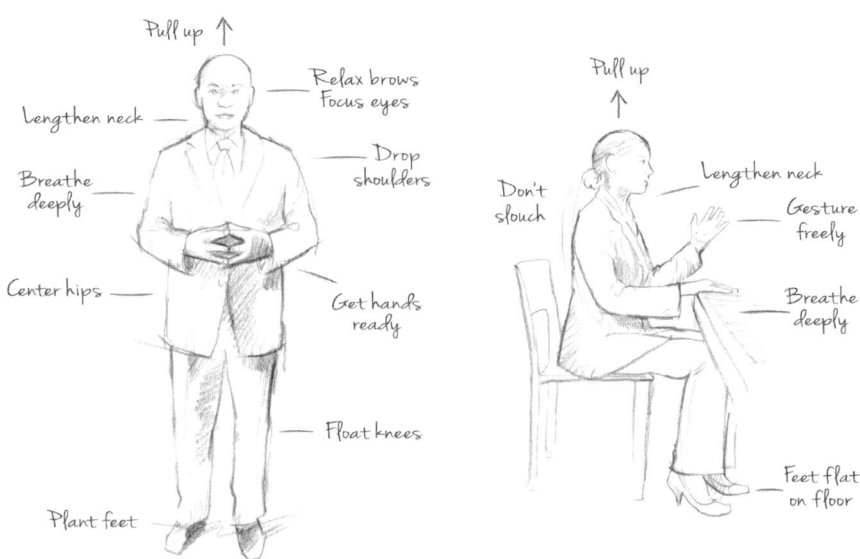

In your practice room, close the door and gain conscious control of your body before you start your practice session. Run your physical checklist, starting with your feet as foundation and moving up the body. If you are practicing for an arbitration, run a similar checklist sitting down. The more you practice your checklist, the more automatic it will become. Eventually your body will align itself before you speak.

Warm Up Your Voice

Stretch your face very wide and stick out your tongue. Then withdraw your tongue and compress all the facial muscles. Stretch and compress these muscles a few times until you can feel the increased blood flow warming your facial muscles.

Repeat these vocal exercises and tongue twisters, overarticulating and increasing your speed as you go:

niminy piminy, niminy piminy, niminy piminy, niminy piminy (etc.)

butta gutta, butta gutta, butta gutta, butta gutta, butta gutta, butta gutta (etc.)

She sells seashells by the seashore.

Three free thugs set three thugs free.

Who What When Where Why Which How

Speak in Phrases

Begin speaking at a pace that immediately captures the deliberate rhythm of speaking in phrases. Americans may imitate the rhythm of the Pledge of Allegiance. Carefully construct your sentences or questions one phrase at a time to give your brain a chance to collaborate with your speaking voice.

If you must begin with a ritual introduction—"May it please the court, your honor, counsel, members of the jury, my name is ..."—use that introductory boilerplate to set a manageable and deliberate pace, just like musicians set the proper tempo for a piece of music.

Gesture Immediately

Open your hands to gesture just before the very first word comes out of your mouth. The flow of your gestures will facilitate the streaming of your thoughts and words. If you are practicing an examination, gesture immediately toward the witness stand using the palm-up, questioning gesture, with one or both hands extended toward your imaginary witness. If you are practicing an opening statement or closing argument, place some initial key words "on the shelf" at waist level.

Talk First and Write Second

To help develop a natural fluidity in your presentation style, try talking first and writing second. Let the speech center of your brain generate what you intend to say. Once you've said it, create the outline. As you rough draft aloud, stop and jot down the ideas you like best. If you like a particular turn of phrase, repeat it several times to promote muscle memory. Add it to your notes so that you can decide later whether to keep it for your final presentation. It can be useful just to free-associate aloud as you begin to shape your motion, appeal, opening statement, or closing argument.

Rough draft aloud what you intend to say; expect it to be uneven and unpolished at first. There is an advantage to finding out what you do *not* want to say. As with writing, you can go back over the draft and keep polishing.

Practice Your Beginning

Given the rule of primacy, pay particular attention to the beginning of your practice topic. Don't waste your time thanking the jury for their service or offering clichés: "This is the opening statement, which is like a road map …" Avoid meaningless filler: "Mr. Harvey, I've just got a few questions …" Practice saying something of interest right at the start, and say it an interesting way. Cut to the chase. Have a dynamic purpose from the very beginning. Start with something that will make the listener want to pay further attention. This is as much a matter of sounding as if you have an interesting purpose as it is of actually having one.

Practice Your Ending

To follow the rule of recency, always end your presentations with clarity and confidence, both substantively and stylistically. Practice the ending several times, until you are confident that it will put a strong finish on your presentation. Make sure to practice what you will ask for in the final paragraph of your motion ("We ask the court to grant …"), opening ("At the end of this trial, I will ask you …"), or closing argument ("Members of the jury, as you deliberate, I ask you to …"). If you genuinely feel the need to thank your jurors for their service, do it in the penultimate position: "Before I conclude, members of the jury, I want to thank you …" An easy way to signal you are nearly done, this guarantees that the jury will attend closely to your conclusion.

Similarly, in examinations, practice the line of questioning that will end your examination. Know and practice your last question in particular. If you haven't planned and practiced your final question, how will you know when your examination is finished? On cross examination, if you have a zinger for a final question, practice setting it up with the phrase, "Just one final question, Mr. Andersen," so the fact finders are alerted that the end is near. The rule of recency says they are likely to remember what you say just before sitting down, so end with something interesting and memorable that advances your case.

Practice Transitions and Headlines

As a separate memory exercise, say aloud the transitions that will move you from topic to topic. The muscle memory from practicing these transitions aloud will help you remember them under pressure. You may choose sometimes to close out a previous topic definitively before announcing the next one, using recency and primacy as a memory aid and attention-grabber for the jury:

> We have discussed what happened on July 15th.
> *(an ending: where you have been)*

Now let's focus on the events of July 17th.
(a new beginning: where you are going)

In a direct examination, you can use the same technique to clarify your structure:

Ms. Wang, we have discussed your educational background *(ending)*;
now let's talk about your professional experience *(beginning)*.

If you remind your listeners where you've been, and tell them where you're going next, they're more likely to know where you are—and to stay with you in the moment.

During cross examination, you usually will be cagier about your structure, to avoid tipping off the witness about where you are going. Therefore, practice the transition from one line of questioning to the next, without the obvious recency/primacy, ending/beginning headlines of direct examination. If, before moving on, you want the jury to think about your previous line of questioning, practice inserting persuasive silence as you transition to the next topic. During this silence you are subliminally suggesting, "Think about that!" Count to yourself two or three seconds of silence to let your listeners think about what the witness just admitted. Let them realize the importance of your previous line of questioning, then move on. Three seconds will feel like a long time, but of course it isn't. If you practice counting the seconds silently, you'll begin to get comfortable with using longer silences for transitions.

Practice Jump-Starting Your Gestures

Practice how you will jump-start your instinct to gesture so that it immediately takes over, freeing you to think about more important things. Decide exactly what you want to say, and then find a gesture appropriate to your words. Place key words "on the shelf." Your emphasis will be reinforced by accompanying gestures at waist height.

When You Must Read Aloud: Practice!

There are times when you need to read from a document. You may read from a report, contract, witness statement, or deposition during impeachment. Resist the temptation to read too fast for your listeners to comprehend. When you must read, here's how to do it effectively:

1. Pick up the document and hold it up. Don't leave it on the lectern.

2. Read it a phrase at a time, emphasizing key words in each phrase.

3. Read the *meaning* of the words, not just the words themselves.

Practice reading aloud slowly and, if you need to, mark up the document to assist your reading. Put slash marks where you intend to pause between phrases, and underline the key words in each phrase that clarify the meaning. A few minutes of practice will ensure that you make the greatest possible impact.

After all, the point of reading any document aloud is to have significant impact—don't leave it to chance. If the quote is complicated, don't hesitate to read it a second time, saying, "Let me read that again." Read it even more deliberately and expressively the second time.

When You Recite from Memory

Sometimes the verbatim repetition of *a phrase or sentence* will be useful, or even necessary, in trial. You may have to quote your client or an opposing party, or refer to the precise language of a contract, letter, e-mail, statement, transcript, or deposition. Practice saying these words until they roll off your tongue easily. Whenever you plan to quote a person or document verbatim, double-check to make sure you have memorized the quotation accurately. It can be very persuasive to quote something precisely from memory, but you must not paraphrase.

Notes and Visual Aids

Once you have structured and practiced your whole presentation, make sure to practice with the final version of your notes. Write legibly and large enough so that your notes are easy to see, whether placed on a lectern or left on the edge of counsel table.

If you plan to use visual aids in a presentation, practice working with them. Make sure they're legible for the listener. If you're going to write on a flip chart, practice writing big, legibly, and carefully. Generally, "jumbo" size marker pens make flip chart visuals vastly easier to read than regular markers.

As you practice speaking with a flip chart, projection screen, or other visual aid, stand with your toes pointed toward your listener. If you point your toes toward the visual aid, you'll end up addressing it instead of the people you want to persuade. Pointing your toes toward the listeners will keep you facing in the right direction. When you gesture to your visual aid, use the arm that is closest to it. When you point to something on the visual aid, leave your hand on the visual aid for reference, but turn your head and eyes back to speak to the listeners. Touch the visual, turn to the listeners, and then talk to them. Think of these as the 3 Ts: touch, turn, talk.

Practice with computer-generated visual aids on a big screen. This will give you a feel for what the viewers will be seeing for the first time. Give them time to absorb what is there. When you want them to read what you've put up on the screen, adjust your pace and rhythm to accommodate them. It is counterproductive to ask them to split their focus between listening to you and looking at the screen. Give them time to read. Tell them what they are looking at:

> This is the emergency room report.

Tell them where on the screen you want them to look:

> Look halfway down the page at the box indicating blood-alcohol level.

Don't talk to the screen; talk to the jury about what is on the screen. If you intend to read from a visual aid, practice reading from it in the same deliberate manner described above.

When you are finished, get rid of the slide by going to a blank slide that will turn your screen blue or black.

Practice Courtroom Rituals Aloud

There are many spoken rituals in the courtroom that require you to say aloud the necessary steps in the proper order, for both the judge and the record. These rituals include the steps to get an exhibit into evidence, or to impeach a witness with a prior inconsistent statement. If you practice these rituals aloud, you will be able to march through the steps with confidence. They should be automatic. For example:

> I am holding what has been pre-marked as Defendant's exhibit number one for identification.
>
> Showing to opposing counsel ...

Your honor, may I approach the witness?

I'm showing you what has been pre-marked as Defendant's exhibit number one for identification.

Do you recognize it?

What is it? (etc.)

Different types of exhibits require different verbal rituals to move them into evidence successfully. Laying the foundation for a photograph is different from laying the foundation for a business record. Practice asking these various foundational questions, in their proper order, until they are automatic. Walk through the steps in your practice space, saying the exact words aloud, as if you were showing the exhibit to opposing counsel and approaching the witness. The more you practice the full routine, actions as well as words, the more your muscle memory will assist you in remembering it under pressure.

Make a Video

There is no feedback more valuable than seeing and hearing yourself as others do. If you have access to a video camera or smartphone that makes video, use it. When you practice, don't speak directly at the camera with your eyes focused on the lens—it is too difficult to keep your concentration while talking to a device. If you are using a chair as a witness stand, place the camera slightly off to the side. Or place the camera where the jury will be sitting to see yourself from their perspective.

When you watch the video, avoid harsh criticism. Don't focus only on what you don't like—see and hear the positive elements as well. One way to be more objective and technical in your self-analysis is to attend to the observable, quantifiable elements of persuasive style: How often do you move your feet? How many steps are you taking per minute? How many seconds do you pause to think or let your jury think? How long does it take for you to use your first gesture? How many seconds do your gestures last? Once you know the numbers, you can set clear goals to walk or shift less often, to pause longer, or to gesture sooner the next time you practice. The Video Self-Review Checklist in Appendix Two will help your evaluation.

Exercises to Solve Specific Problems

"I talk too softly."

If you talk too softly, practice taking deeper abdominal breaths both before and while you are speaking. Slow your pace deliberately to give yourself time to draw in longer, larger breaths between sentences. Practice speaking a sentence at a time, stopping to take a deeper breath at the ends of sentences. Because emphatic words are louder, emphasize at least one key word in every phrase. Remember to gesture as you practice, to get the feel for how language is tied to moving hands.

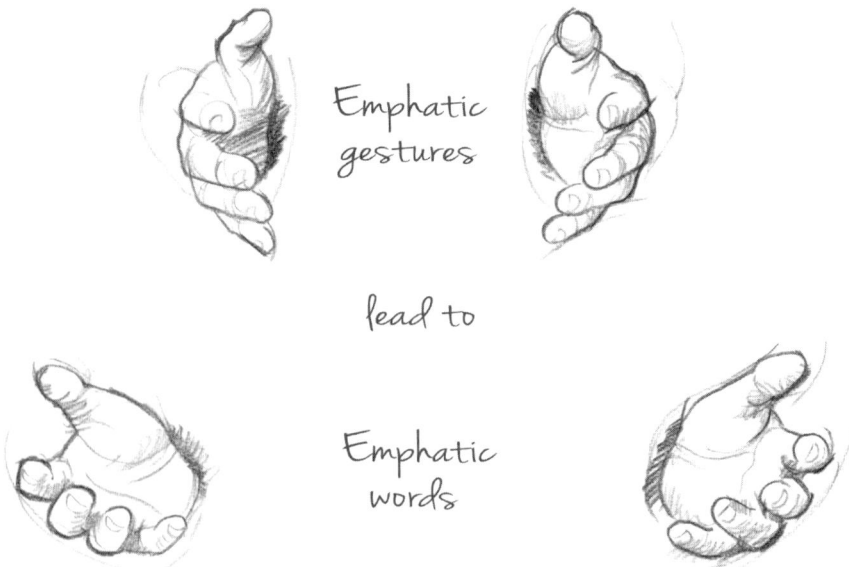

Soft-spoken people tend to trail off on the final phrase or word of a sentence or question. To counter this tendency, speak more loudly as you approach the ends of sentences or questions. Deliberately stress the final word of each sentence. Tell yourself to be louder at the end. This will keep the volume consistent throughout the utterance.

"I just can't stand still."

Stand up and consciously feel the soles of your feet inside your shoes. Wiggle your toes. Feel your feet in contact with the floor, which sits upon the foundation of the building, which is planted on the earth. Your pedestal is the whole planet; feel yourself anchored to it. Do not move your feet as you start to talk. Inhibit the instinct to talk and walk simultaneously. Keep your feet planted as you begin to speak, and let your arms do the walking.

Gesture immediately. Although physical energy naturally seeks a path that leads downward, through your legs, send the energy into your arms instead. Once your arms are gesturing properly, your voice will be more expressive, too.

At first, practice saying only a single paragraph or topic without moving your feet; gradually work up to doing an entire opening or closing standing in one place. Once you can stand still, practice using a limited number of moves as transitions between topics. During an opening, for example, stand in one place to talk about your client, and then move to a different location to discuss the opposing party. Shift a third time to conclude. Practice using a limited number of moves for transitions between topics in examinations.

"I speak too quickly."

Speaking too quickly is merely a habit, and habits can be broken. Practice speaking in phrases while attending to the short silences separating your phrases and sentences. Before you speak, take a deep breath and concentrate on hearing the silence in the room. When you speak, exploit this silence. Begin speaking, and immediately insert silence between your first phrases. When you come to the end of a sentence, stop for a longer span of time than your instincts might dictate. Imagine that the period at the end of the sentence is a stoplight, and that you plan to sit silently at that stoplight for a short while. Focus less on the speed at which you are talking than on the gaps between phrases when you are *not* talking.

To discover a suitable rhythm, say aloud the phrases below. Hear the silence before and between the phrases:

> Your only goal *(Silence)* while speaking *(Silence)* is to hear the silence *(Silence)* between the phrases. *(Silence)*

Use that pace as you practice. Once you can hear the silence, notice how much easier it is to speak when you give yourself time to think. Simply shorten the silent gaps between phrases and sentences until you find the appropriate pace for speaking as an advocate. This is an exercise, not an attempt to find a conversational pace. Once you know how to slow yourself down, you can pick up the tempo again.

"My eyes aren't focused."

Make it your ritual to focus first and talk second. Don't speak until your gaze is fixed on an imaginary witness, judge, arbitrator, or jury across the room. Speak aloud as you continue to intentionally focus your eyes. When you find your eyes wandering—perhaps looking toward the floor or ceiling as you pause to think—be aware of breaking eye contact and return to your original point of focus. Look directly at your imaginary witness as you practice asking questions of him. Draw a life-size pair of eyes on a piece of paper and tape them to the chair. Focus on them as you ask questions. Identify the area where your imaginary jury is sitting, and speak to them. Use a couple of chairs to indicate the ends of the jury box. As you practice, make roving eye contact with the imaginary individual jurors seated within that perimeter.

"I say *um* too much."

To eliminate the *um* habit, substitute silence in its place. Choose a topic that's familiar and ordinary, and begin talking. Describe what you did last weekend. Talk about what you did on your last vacation. Speak at full voice; don't mumble. As you talk aloud, your only goals are to speak in phrases and to mind the gaps between phrases and sentences. The pace isn't important, the silence is. Your aim is to activate your awareness of thinking noises and the silences that will replace them.

Before you begin, hear the silence around you. Start talking, and insert silence into the gaps between phrases and sentences. Here is a typographical example of the pace:

> Last weekend ... *(mind the gap)*
> I was extremely busy ... *(mind the gap)*
> and I didn't stop for a minute. *(mind the gap)*
> When I awoke on Saturday ... *(mind the gap)*
> the first thing I needed to do ... *(mind the gap)*
> was to run some errands ... *(mind the gap)*
> and get my oil changed. *(mind the gap)*

When you use a thinking noise, hear it and take note of it, but don't stop to chastise yourself. Such a deeply ingrained, persistent habit will continue to appear periodically. Continue speaking, with your goal being to speak for longer and longer stretches without saying *um* or *uh*. When you hear one, be mindful of it, and avoid using it as you go forward.

Once you have free-associated about last weekend or your vacation, repeat this exercise but speak about a topic related to the law. Use one that is currently on your mind or on your desk. Explain something legal. Talk about what "beyond a reasonable doubt" or "preponderance of the evidence" means. Explain the difference between a trademark and a copyright. Imagine yourself teaching the meaning of a legal concept or term to someone who isn't a lawyer—just as you will need to teach facts to the judge, jury, or arbitrator. Again, the subject is less important than your awareness of minding the gaps between phrases.

Keep your practice sessions short; initially, just five to ten minutes is best. Gradually, lengthen the time you are able to speak with articulate control and without thinking noises. Practice longer presentations, such as an opening or closing. Once you have developed sufficient awareness, the next step is to practice conversation without thinking noises. Use silence instead of *um* in more casual settings. The more you do this, the sooner you'll develop a new habit: the habit of speaking without thinking noises. Once you can do this in conversation, it is relatively easy to do so as an advocate.

"I say *okay* after answers on direct examination."

Many lawyers unconsciously say *okay* after a witness gives an answer during direct examination. Like all habits, this reflexive use of *okay* is difficult to break, for several reasons. *Okay* is the expression we use in conversation to affirm that we are listening and understanding. We nod; we say *uh-huh, mmmmmm,* or *okay*. Practitioners unconsciously reinforce this habit by saying *okay* repeatedly while taking depositions.

You can't eliminate this habit by giving yourself the negative instruction "Stop saying *okay!*" Your brain does not respond well to these admonitions, especially when it's unaware of inserting *okay* in the first place. If you were aware of saying it, you would stop. Rather than trying to attack this habit directly, examine your timing—focus on exactly when you say *okay*. It happens immediately after your witness finishes an answer. *Okay* pops out of your mouth before you have time to monitor it, much less eliminate it. It sounds like this:

Q: What do you do for a living?
A: I'm a plumber.
Q: *Okay* ... How long have you been a plumber?
A: Twenty years.
Q: *Okay* ... Who do you work for?
A: Myself.
Q: *Okay* ...

Since *okay* happens right after the answer, focus your attention on that moment. As soon as the witness finishes speaking, inhale. *Okay* cannot slip out while a breath is slipping in. It takes about one second to fill your lungs with air, the same amount of time it takes to say *okay*. During that time, let your jury think about the witness's answer while you formulate your next question. As you inhale, think of the first word of your next question. It is not *okay*, but rather *who, what, when, where, why, which, how, describe, explain,* or *tell*.

Practice your direct examination aloud, addressing the witness chair in your imaginary courtroom. Inhale intentionally before each question. Train your body to inhale reflexively after the witness finishes an answer. This new habit *(inhale)* will displace the old habit *(okay)*. Try playing both roles in your practice session: ask the question, and then provide the answer you think the witness will give. Between the answer and your next question, consciously inhale. You'll know you are making progress when your lips form the word *okay*, but you catch yourself before it pops out. Be ready to stop yourself when you reach that stage.

"I begin leading questions with *And ...* on cross examination."

Leading questions on cross examination often begin with the conjunction *and*, which is then sometimes followed by a thinking noise: *And ... uh ....* This is a common verbal habit, similar to saying *okay* during direct examination. The word *and* slips out before the advocate is even aware of it, much less able to suppress it:

> Q: You are a plumber, right?
> A: Yes.
> Q: *And ...* you've been a plumber for twenty years, true?
> A: Yes.
> Q: *And ... uh ...* you work for yourself?
> A: Yes.
> Q: *And ... uh ...*

In natural conversation, we frequently link sentences with the conjunction *and*. It is a common, deeply ingrained verbal habit, which is why your brain is primed to insert *and* between questions on cross examination. As with other habits, such as *okay*, you can't eliminate this habit by giving yourself the negative instruction "Don't say *and*!" Give yourself a positive instruction; substitute a conscious breath. You say *and* or *and uh* immediately after your witness has answered your question. As soon as the witness finishes the answer, inhale. *And* cannot slip out while the breath is slipping in.

Practice saying aloud the leading questions in your cross examination. Consciously inhale before asking each question, training your body to inhale reflexively before each question. Play both roles and answer your own question aloud. After you have answered yes or no, inhale before asking the next question.

"I'm so boring."

Tackle this problem in two ways. If possible, watch yourself on video. Evaluate whether your face is a mask of seriousness or if you speak with no attitude or feeling.

First, fix your face. Alter your brow, eyes, and lips to achieve neutral alert, as discussed in Chapter One. If your brow is furrowed, relax it. Raise your eyebrows and part your lips.

Now, ask yourself what your face tells the listener. Pick an attitude. Are you curious? Interested? Eager? The default advocacy attitude is austere, solemn, and somber—something that could be described as Lawyer Gothic, or simply Dead on Arrival. Unrelenting austerity is rarely a compelling or interesting human attitude. Refer to the list of attitudes in Chapter Two to reenergize your demeanor. Pick an attitude to suit your tactics.

One simple way to find a more interesting attitude is to ask yourself, "What is the feeling or attitude I wish to provoke?" In opening statement, use one attitude when you talk about your client and another when you talk about the opposing party. In a serious personal injury case, you would use one attitude to describe how great life was for your client before the accident: "He used to run five miles every day." Use a different attitude to describe how grim life has become since the accident: "Now he can't stand up without help." On direct examination, practice curiosity—let the jury know your witness is interesting. If you want the jury to feel skeptical about a witness on cross, adopt skepticism. Or kill the witness with kindness, at least at the beginning, and get tough later on. Practice your closing argument, adopting specific attitudes: plead, beg, and cajole with your arguments. Be indignant, surprised, befuddled, skeptical.

Informal Practice Sessions

The various practice sessions suggested above are all relatively formal. When you practice aloud in a room alone, you simulate the reality of the proceeding. These practice sessions are essential, but they are by no means your only opportunities to practice. You can also create informal practice sessions to improve your skills. These informal sessions don't allow you to practice all skills simultaneously, but they can be very useful for coordinating your brain and speaking voice.

Here are some suggestions for informal practice:

1. Practice speaking aloud while driving in your car. Although you shouldn't practice gesturing when behind the wheel, drive time offers a good opportunity to practice such verbal skills as eliminating thinking noises, speaking too quickly, or speaking too softly. Discipline yourself to practice for a set amount of time—say, ten minutes. Be uninhibited. If you are driving to a hearing, this kind of practice is especially valuable; it serves as your verbal warm-up. Your self-confidence will be much greater if you know that you've already practiced a number of times that day.

2. Practice speaking aloud while walking for exercise. You'll be in good company: Abraham Lincoln practiced this way. According to historian Harold Holzer, "To familiarize himself with the speech, he took to reciting passages aloud as he walked down the streets of Springfield." This is a good time to rough draft aloud your opening statement or closing argument. Start by practicing discrete moments, such as the first or the final paragraph of your opening or closing. Test out alternative themes this way.

3. Practice speaking aloud during your morning routine on days when you must speak publicly. As you shower or make coffee, practice saying aloud what you must say under pressure later that day. Give your brain and voice a chance to get warmed up hours before you must speak under pressure. This type of practice develops muscle memory, which is extremely helpful. When possible, practice speaking aloud right before you have to perform. Step into a nearby empty room, a deserted stairwell, or even an unoccupied restroom, and say your first sentences aloud. You will be primed and ready to go.

Practice During Everyday Conversations

Every time you speak, you have an opportunity to be articulate and understandable. It is especially easy and useful to practice when you aren't feeling the pressure to perform. In casual chats with friends and colleagues, practice eliminating thinking noises. In personal conversations, slow down your pace and speak in phrases. In meetings or classes, push yourself to ask a question or volunteer an observation as a brief test of your speaking skills under pressure.

To prepare for the challenge of direct examination, ask open-ended questions in conversation. Ask questions that begin with *who, what, when, where, why, which, how, describe, explain,* or *tell.* Not only will you be a more engaging conversational partner, you will also develop the ability to draw information out of another person while directing the conversation—a crucial skill in direct examination.

Observe, Adapt, Adopt

Steal ideas from good role models. Adapt or adopt some of the elements of their style and make them your own. When you hear truly excellent speakers, look and listen closely to understand why they make such a strong impression. Listen to their pacing. How much do they use silence? Watch their eyes. Look at their gestures. Could you adapt a particularly effective gesture and make it your own? Expanding your gestural vocabulary is like expanding your verbal vocabulary; just as you can learn a new word and use it tellingly, you can learn a new gesture and make it part of your personal style.

When you hear mediocre speakers, ask yourself why they make a poor impression. Count the thinking noises. Determine if the pace is too fast. Note those elements of style that you want to avoid in your own delivery, and practice doing the opposite.

The Law of Opposites

As you hone your style, become aware of its individual elements. Perhaps you speak with volume and authority and are an articulate but fast talker. You gesture regularly as part of emphasizing key words. Simply put, you are loud, fast, and animated. These are all good things to have as elements of your personal style, but it is possible to have too much of a good thing. Contrast and variety will best be achieved if you tell yourself periodically that in addition to being loud, fast, and animated, you can also be softer, slower, and still. Invoke the law of opposites, and allow your loud voice to be softer at times, your fast delivery slower, and your animated gestures still.

When you obey the law of opposites, you suddenly have twice as many skills to call upon. Rather than just playing to your strengths—loud, fast, animated—you also play against them. This keeps your delivery interesting. The listener then anticipates the next surprise and contrast, rather than feeling barraged by the same stylistic elements. Human beings crave variety. We quickly tire of the same old thing repeated over and over again. This is especially true of style. Surprise your listener and mix up your choices to keep your voice and presentation from becoming predictable, repetitive, and—ultimately—boring.

When you go in an unexpected stylistic direction, you gain a new expressive capacity. The power of the unobvious choice—of doing what was not foreseen—is its ability to mark important words, phrases, sentences, and questions. If your style is loud, fast, and animated, you can't very well highlight important points by being even louder, faster, and more animated. That would be too much! Instead, choose from a broader range of stylistic elements. Ask yourself, "What is the opposite of my usual demeanor?" Add an exotic spice to a favorite recipe. You need just a dash of soft, slow, and still, not a personality transplant or a radical change of delivery.

Practice making such uncharacteristic choices before trying this technique under pressure. With practice, you will find that your stylistic vocabulary has widened and that you can make novel choices spontaneously. Like a skilled jazz musician, you will learn to live in the present and feel when a choice is instinctively right.

Practicing for the Mental Game

Finding your rituals, developing a solid technique, and relying on good speaking habits all go a long way toward helping you feel prepared to walk into the courtroom. Psyching yourself up for trial, rather than psyching yourself out, is one last critical part of your technique. You have to play the "head game" successfully if you strive to anticipate and look forward to the pressure of performing as an advocate. Mental preparation is as much a matter of technique and practice as eliminating thinking noises or learning to stand still. Each advocate has unique challenges in getting ready.

Here are some ways to think about how to practice for the mental game.

1. Psych yourself up. Litigators engage in a competitive battle of wits. There is a winner, a loser, and a judge as referee. To play to win, psych yourself up before competing, just as athletes do. Athletes chant, shout, and supportively slap each other to get psyched up. Pump yourself up as part of your technique: "I can do this! I can win." Confidence is based on preparation. Tell yourself, "I'm ready. I've practiced. I've done everything I can to prepare. Now, I want to win." Use the techniques in this book to be prepared. Then, you can psych yourself up, not out.

If you have ever had a really unpleasant speaking experience, you may suffer from PTSD, or "post-traumatic speaking disorder." Perhaps you blanked while speaking to your peers in law school, college, or even earlier in your life. Does that one bad experience haunt you still? If so, it is time to get over it.

Make a video while practicing and review it using the Video Self-Review Checklist in Appendix Two. Watch and listen, focusing on the positive elements of style. On a piece of paper, tally the things you already do that work well. Be specific: "I stand still. I don't say *um*. I gesture naturally. I don't appear nervous." Build your newfound confidence on that foundation. Don't be overly critical of the things you don't like or waste negative energy on things you can't change: "I should lose weight" or "My eyes are too close together." That behavior psyches you out. Stop it.

The next time you have to perform, study that list of positive things and tell yourself, "Here's what I do that works." Focus on those positive elements of your style—and you will gradually overcome PTSD, putting it behind you forever.

2. Overcome anxiety. Advocacy can trigger deeply personal issues and anxieties. Some lawyers confess they hate being the center of attention. Others don't like to be stared at intensely. Still others don't like making eye contact with strangers. Some are uncomfortable mustering the assertiveness required for cross examination; it feels too aggressive and domineering.

If you are dealing with any of these issues, you can change. Make a conscious decision to work on your personal anxiety. Pinpoint what bothers you the most, practice that specific skill, and become comfortable doing it.

3. Practice breathing. Of all the techniques in this book, the practice of conscious breathing is both the most important, and also the most undervalued. As you prepare for a trial, deliberate breathing can help to turn off unhelpful thoughts of negative anticipation. When the bailiff calls, "All rise!" and you know you are about to begin a trial, breathing is the last thing you can do to keep your wits about you. The more you employ this technique, the better it works. If you focus on conscious breathing in the moment, you won't focus on fretting about the future, you'll be psyching yourself up to perform.

Summary

Practice is the only way to improve any skill. It is the ultimate skill, allowing you to turn what you know into the solid performance skill of know-how. Conquer any resistance you may feel about practicing and learn to do it alone, aloud, and a lot. Remember, you are not prepping yourself to be perfect; you are practicing to get better. Be patient and methodical. It doesn't have to take hours every day. Short sessions may be more productive.

Create notes to serve as a visual aid that will allow you to refine the skill of structured improvisation. As you begin, run up your body's checklist from feet to head. Warm up your articulators so those muscles are ready to work. Give special energy and attention to rehearsing beginnings and endings. Once you decide what you wish to say to begin, train yourself to jump-start your instinct to gesture.

Practice with your visual aids, and if you intend to read from a document, read it numerous times, deliberately and with meaning. If you have a particular skill you are attempting to improve, take ten minutes a day to focus exclusively on that skill.

In addition to formal practice sessions, use speaking opportunities in everyday life—informal practice—to improve your ability to communicate fluently and articulately. Carefully observe other advocates and public speakers; adopt and adapt the skills you see used by gifted communicators. Understand and avoid those problems that make mediocre speakers less effective. Psych yourself up to speak. Discover the excitement and satisfaction in doing it well.

Practice really does work, producing tangible results in a surprisingly short time. Ask any professional athlete or musician. If you've managed to read this far without actually trying any of the exercises suggested, put down the book and give it a whirl.

Talk to Yourself

"Just five minutes of practice builds confidence."

"Practice out loud using these notes to make sure they work."

"I'm stuck in traffic! Practice the beginning of my speech again."

"Eliminate *um* and think in silence."

"Be more aware of my eye contact during this lunch with colleagues."

"Walk down the steps to sound confident during this phone call."

"Talking too fast is just a habit. Speak in phrases instead."

"Practice the conclusion so I can jump to it if I run out of time."

Chapter Five
Applying Your Skills at Trial

This chapter will integrate the delivery skills you have learned and combine them with the unique requirements for each phase of trial. Now is the time to put it all together, coordinating your body, brain, and voice with the speechmaking of opening or closing, and the questioning skills needed for jury selection, direct examination, and cross examination. For maximum benefit, stand up and get the feel of the physical behaviors described. The speaking skills, such as the many variations for the proper form of questions, can be assimilated while sitting down, as long as you say each variation out loud.

Jury Selection

Because first impressions are so important, you want to begin making that positive impression during jury selection. It is your first opportunity to connect with the panel and those people who will ultimately sit on the jury. Before speaking to them, select the attitude, tone, and demeanor with which you will introduce yourself. The energy and attitude you use for this in a professional setting are appropriate and natural for a trial situation.

If you want the panel to be open with you, you need to be open with them—in a literal sense. Openness is a two-way street, and you need to go first. Do not cower behind the lectern, staring down at your legal pad. Step away, look your listeners in the eyes, and gesture expansively. Loosen up. Don't clasp your hands together protectively below the waist in the "fig leaf" position. Before you begin to speak, lift your hands to the ready position at waist height. Gesture immediately as you introduce yourself; this will help you loosen up and open up.

Deliver your introduction without looking at notes. Prepare and practice it in advance. Knowing exactly what to say at the beginning will bolster your confidence, and it will free you to make panoramic eye contact with everyone on the panel. Offer a short explanation of the process and what you are attempting to do. Explain that you are seeking to pick the right jurors for this particular case. Give them a specific example of what you mean: a person recently injured in a car crash, obviously, wouldn't be the right juror in a case involving a car accident. Tell them you don't mean to pry. Explain the option of answering privately in chambers. Keep it short.

Be open   Not closed

Call on individuals using *Mr., Mrs.,* and *Ms.* and their last names, or *sir* and *ma'am*. Create a seating chart with last names that are written large and easy to read. Hold the seating chart down at your side when you are not looking at it; don't gesture with it or hold it like a protective shield in front of you. When asking questions of the whole panel, instruct them as to how they should respond, such as "Please raise your hand to answer."

The process of jury selection varies depending on the jurisdiction. Sometimes the judge may ask all the questions. Find out in advance how jury selection works where you practice. When you are allowed to question the panel, here is one technique to get the panel talking about the issues you need to explore:

1. Announce a topic relevant to the case.

2. Suggest a wide range of feelings about that topic.

3. Ask for individual responses.

4. Use open-ended questions to learn more.

5. Pose leading questions to conclude.

For example, if a traffic accident case involves texting while driving, this is how the pattern might work:

1. Announce a topic. "This case involves texting while driving."

2. Suggest a range of feelings. "Some people, on the one hand, think that texting while driving is extremely dangerous and never do it. On the other hand, there are drivers who think it is safe and do it all the time."

3. Ask for individual responses. Select a panelist and ask, "How do you feel about texting and driving, Ms. Escobar?" Once you get an answer, you can turn randomly to another person and ask, "Do you feel differently, Mr. Willis?" or "Do you share that feeling, Ms. Long?" or "How about you, Mrs. Goldstein?" An unpredictable pattern of calling on people keeps the whole panel alert, ready, and even eager to answer. This works better than moving down the row predictably and asking each person in turn. To make sure you've invited everyone to talk, ask, "Does anyone else have personal feelings about this issue?"

Depending on your case, this pattern works for many issues and topics—big corporations, insurance companies, large jury verdicts, motorcycles, guns, alcohol, contractors, infidelity, and so on. In a medical malpractice case, the topic might be doctors. "This case involves a doctor. Some folks hold doctors in very high esteem; others have been harmed while under a doctor's care. How do you feel about doctors, sir?" It gets the conversation rolling. Once they are talking, you have specific information to develop so you can dig deeper.

There is an obvious gesture pattern that works with this technique. Using the double karate chop gesture, place the topic "on the shelf" directly in front of you: "This case involves texting while driving."

Place the range of responses on either side, gesturing with one hand for the positive feeling and the other hand for the negative feeling. Consider the issues in your case and develop the topics that work with this pattern. Then practice saying the pattern out loud while gesturing.

4. Use open-ended questions. Once a panel member has revealed strong feelings about a topic, you may need to probe for more details. Just as you will do during direct examination, use open-ended questions to elicit information. Start questions with *who, what, when, where, why, which,* or *how*. Use polite commands to get more details.

Describe that experience.

Explain further what you mean.

Tell me about those feelings.

Elaborate on that.

Be aware that questions beginning with a verb will often elicit only a *yes* or *no* answer. "Did you think …?" "Do you find …?" "Were you able …?" "Can you promise …?" They will reveal less about a person.

5. Pose leading questions. Conclude the questioning of a given individual with leading questions. "You clearly feel very strongly about this, am I correct? Do you think it would be hard to set that feeling aside? Given that experience, could you be fair as a juror in this case?"

When you get an honest, revealing answer, reward that candor. The panel may be more willing to talk to you about personal prejudices or strong biases if you acknowledge their honesty:

I am grateful for your candor.

Thank you for being open about that.

I appreciate your honesty.

Your frankness is commendable.

Opening Statement

To deliver a persuasive opening, have a clear understanding of the difference between stating a fact and arguing a conclusion. You begin the trial with opening *statement*. You state what you expect the facts will be during the trial. It is not an opening *argument* during which you argue inferences and conclusions based on those facts. Not only is it against the rules to argue, but it is also presumptuous to do so regarding facts not yet in evidence. Trial lawyers do this far too often—and often get away with it. One simple way to avoid arguing during opening is to ask yourself these questions as you practice out loud: Is what I'm saying a fact taken from a witness statement, deposition, expert opinion, document, or exhibit? Or is this an inference or conclusion I have drawn myself from the facts? If it is an inference or conclusion, it belongs in closing argument.

Another thing you must avoid in opening is asking the jurors to place themselves in the position of one of the parties. You cannot ask the jury, "What would you have done if you were in that same situation, members of the jury?" You cannot say, "She did what you and I would have done." In addition, you cannot personally vouch for witnesses or facts. Also be wary of the personal pronoun "I" and phrases like "I think" or "I believe." The objection to this violation of the rules is "Objection, *unethical!*" You don't want to hear that from opposing counsel, and it is likely to be sustained. Stick to the facts.

Avoid starting your opening with the clichés so popular with ineffective advocates: "Opening statement is like a road map…" Does any juror get excited about road maps? "This is like the table of contents…" Is there anything less compelling than a table of contents? Assuming you were introduced earlier or questioned the panel during jury selection, you don't need to reintroduce yourself. They know who you are, so get on with it.

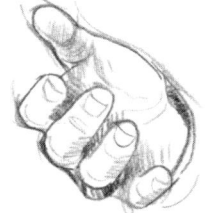 

Start your opening statement with a theme that captures your theory of the case. Say something compelling in an interesting manner, and use gestures that will appropriately suit your theme. Be sure to practice the words with the gestures together ahead of time. Here are some examples of themes:

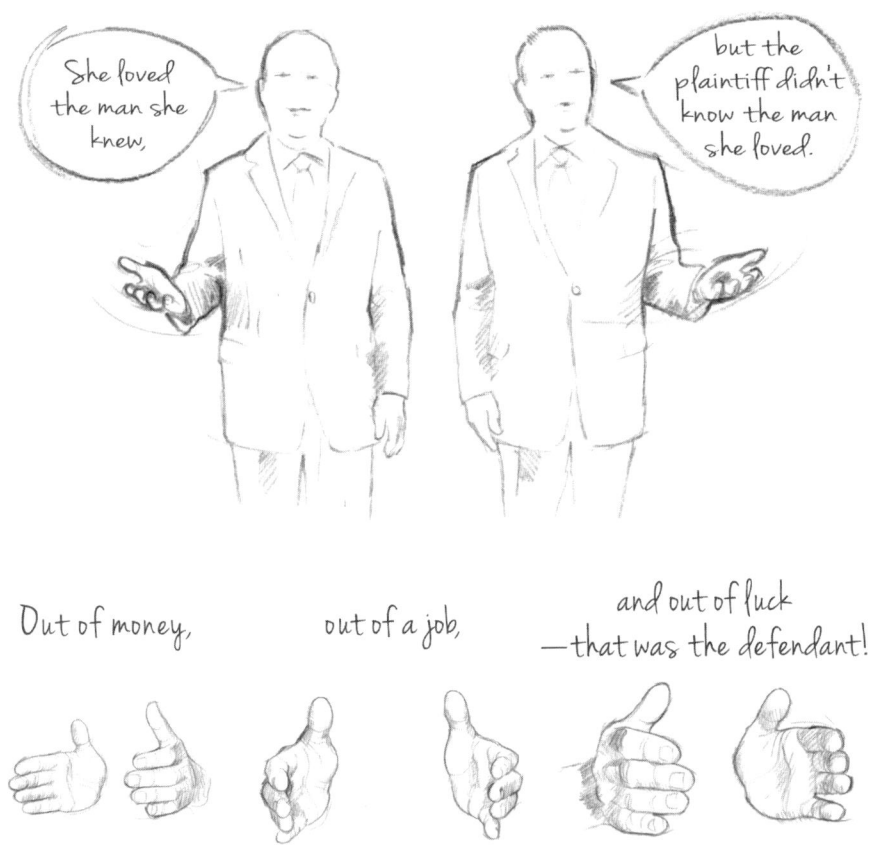

As you proceed through your opening, be careful to limit how many times you say, "The evidence will show …" Opening statement is implicitly what the evidence will show. It is tiresome to hear this unnecessary phrase over and over again—better to be specific about what you mean. Preview for the jury how the evidence will show a given fact or who will do it.

The defendant will sit right there on the witness stand and admit ...

You will read the language in the contract.

An accident reconstruction expert will show you exactly how it happened.

You will see the gun used in the robbery.

Select the appropriate attitude for speaking about your client, and use a different one for speaking about the opposing side. Just as your voice and demeanor would be different when talking about your best friend versus a complaining neighbor, pick the attitude that fits the party.

Grab your jurors' attention by starting with a dynamic and confident volume, then periodically surprise them with the contrast of speaking softer yet audibly. Variety of delivery is essential to holding jurors' attention. Vary your pace and volume to emphasize the most important facts. Just as you use yellow highlighter on a page, say key facts in a way that signals their importance. Speak more slowly, more emphatically, or even softer on the facts you want the jury to remember. Pause briefly after a vital fact to let it sink in. Use this persuasive silence to give the jury time to think about and process what you have said.

If you feel strongly that you need to thank the jury for their service, save it for the end of your opening statement. Don't start by thanking them just because someone told you to do so. It will sound canned and insincere; it is difficult to sound sincere at the start. If you wait until the end, however, you will be warmed up and appear genuine. Just before your concluding thought, say, "Before I finish, I want to thank you for your service." This also signals that you are about to wrap up. This is advantageous, because jurors will be paying close attention when you explain what you will ask them to do at the conclusion of the trial:

At the end of this trial I am going to ask you to find in favor of ...

After you have heard all the evidence, I will ask you …

Be sure to sustain your energy, volume, and confidence all the way through the final consonant of the last word. Don't fade away on the final phrase. Practice your last sentence repeatedly until it trips off your tongue effortlessly.

I will ask you to find for the plaintiff.

I will ask you to find for the defendant.

I will ask you to find for the prosecution.

Before trial, practice your opening statement out loud while using a timer. Especially if the judge has restricted the amount of time you have, you want to know how long your statement will last. You cannot accurately guess the length of your opening by the number of PowerPoint slides or pages of notes you have prepared. Remember that brevity is a virtue. It's better to be shorter than too long.

Direct Examination

If you want the jury to be curious and interested in what your witness has to say, you need to sound equally curious and interested yourself as you ask questions. Since you already know all the answers and have no genuine curiosity about them, it's possible to sound bored and indifferent. Think about and select your attitude to be a role model for the curiosity and interest you want the jury to feel in response to your witness. Different topics and different lines of questions may require a shift in your attitude.

Direct is not simply a one-on-one conversation with the witness. It is a presentation to the court. Speak loudly enough to be heard by everyone, and instruct your witness to do the same. Raising your level of curiosity will naturally increase your energy and volume.

Another technique is to emphatically stress at least one word in each question you ask. This will help clarify the meaning of the question and boost your volume.

What *time* did you leave?

Who *else* was at the meeting?

How *closely* did you read the contract?

Which car had the red light?

You may be tempted to overuse questions like "What happened next?" and "What did you do next?" These questions are technically objectionable because they call for a narrative. But the real problem with these types of questions is that they put you at risk of losing control of the direct. The witness may tell the whole story in a way that is not persuasive or clear. Limit the time frame of the question to indicate to the witness that you want a short answer and not a long narrative:

What was the very next thing that happened?

What was the very next thing you did?

What was the first thing that happened after that?

What was the first thing you did then?

Be mindful that direct is about helping connect your witness to the fact finder. Triangulate the conversation. It has three points: you, your witness, and the jury. Acknowledge that the most important person or people in the room are the fact finders by using phrases such as "Tell us …," "Tell her honor …," "Explain to the court …," and "Define for the jury …."

Be sure to look over at the jury occasionally. Once in a while, start questioning while looking at the witness, glance casually at the jury in the middle of the question, and then return to your witness at the end. This is a variation of the eye contact you make when conversing with several people at once; you look at each of them in turn, for at least some of the time. Do this with jurors, especially on important questions. Attention is reciprocal. If you pay attention to them, they are more likely to pay attention to your questions and your witness's answers.

During direct, you want to make the witness the star. The operative word here is *make*. Like the film director on a movie set, you are the director of the direct exam. Don't be misled by clichés suggesting that, as a direct examiner, you need to disappear or become wallpaper. This implies that you lower your energy during direct, which doesn't work very well. Film directors don't disappear as they direct; they take charge and make the star look good. To do this, raise your energy, but direct it toward the witness. Make sure the witness is talking more and you are talking less. Use open-ended questions to help with this.

To prime your brain to ask open-ended questions on direct, recite aloud these words: *Who? What? When? Where? Why? Which? How?* Say them again until you memorize them. These are the questioning words that get a witness talking. (Notice how all these words make your lips go round as you say them.) Repeat them until they are imprinted on your muscle memory. To form open-ended questions, these seven words are most often placed at the beginning:

Who was the owner?

What did he hand you?

When did you arrive?

Where did she take you?

Why did you go there?

Which car had the green light?

How did you pay him?

They may also occur at the end:

The owner was *who*?

He handed you *what*?

You arrived *when*?

She took you *where*?

You went there *why*?

The light was green for *which* car?

You paid him *how*?

In addition to questioning words, use commands:

Describe that intersection.

Explain the difference, doctor, between a laminectomy and laminotomy.

Tell us the reason you did not respond.

Define that term for us.

Calculate the amount of lost revenue.

A film director instructs the movie star when to back up or move forward. You can use a similar technique with your witness. These commands will help you achieve this goal:

Stop right there, and tell us what you were thinking.

Back up to the night before the surgery.

Fast forward to the moment right before you heard the explosion.

Because you already know the answers on direct, you may be tempted, unconsciously, to ask leading questions. They are sometimes allowed during direct, if what you are asking about is preliminary, not in dispute, and will move the testimony along. Because direct is smoother when you ask open-ended questions, make sure you know exactly what type of question you are asking, every time. Paying attention to grammar quickly becomes second nature. As with jury selection, be careful about asking a series of questions that begin with verbs, as in

Did you …?

Were you …?

Can you ...?

Have you ...?

These questions call for a *yes* or *no* answer. You will be doing most of the talking, not the witness. In the following examples, see how the phrasing of the question affects who provides the critical detail:

Q: Did you provide the bank with designs, customer lists, and marketing studies?

A: Yes.

versus

Q: What did you provide the bank?

A: I gave them designs, customer lists, and marketing studies.

Bear in mind the jury has been told that what the lawyers say—what *you* say—is not evidence. Therefore, make sure the important evidence comes from the witness in an answer, and not from you in your question.

To complicate this issue of how to form questions, starting with a verb can land you somewhere in between open-ended and leading. For example, this verb-start question doesn't suggest an answer:

Did he have a valid driver's license?

He did or he did not—*yes* or *no*. But the following verb-start question definitely suggests an answer.

Did he appear to be extremely drunk?

Make sure the form of your question—open-ended, leading, or verb-start—fits your tactical goal during direct. Forming the right question is a challenging skill. Everyday conversation does not require that people think about grammar, semantics, and syntax. It isn't natural, and it isn't easy for many advocates. Practice aloud using the right form of question until you get comfortable doing so.

As you ask questions, use the questioning gesture. This palms-up gesture, done with one or both hands, will add energy, emphasis, and curiosity to your delivery. It also directs the focus of the jury toward the witness.

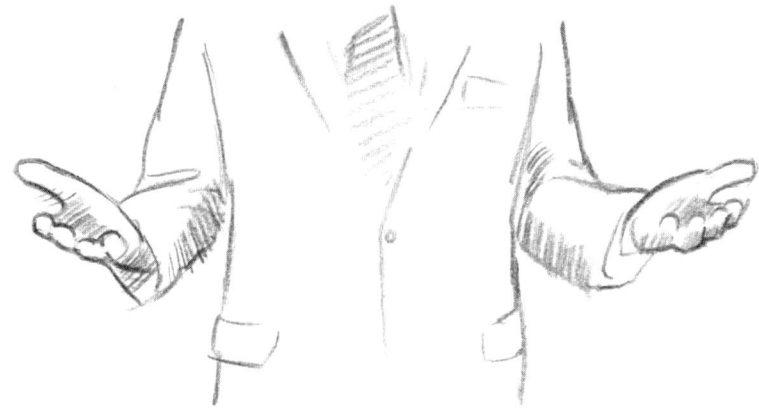

A good direct takes advantage of headlining or head-noting each line of questioning. This will mentally focus your witness, your fact finder, and yourself by stating each specific topic before asking questions about it. Just as a film director chooses where to focus the camera, you focus on a topic.

Let's focus on the night before the incident.

Let's focus on that July 13th meeting.

Let's focus on how you tied the suture.

Alternatively, you can phrase headlines like this:

Let's talk about the weather the day of the accident.

Let's explore the risks involved in that procedure.

Let's delve into the nonobvious elements of your patent.

Cross Examination

If your witness is the star on direct, you are the star on cross. Take command of the courtroom. The focus is on you, so do not slouch on the lectern, bury your nose in your notes, and read your questions. Raise your energy and your volume and talk to the witness and *through* the witness to the jury.

Pick the appropriate attitude for different lines of questioning on cross. Do not default to hostility and aggression. The adversarial nature of cross makes this surprisingly instinctive and easy to do, but your cross needn't sound *cross*. Nothing will surprise your witness more than if you are polite and friendly as you begin. The witness will have a much harder time fighting with you. If you want a witness to agree, sound agreeable. You attract more flies with honey than with vinegar, as the old saying goes. Start agreeably and become more aggressive, if you need to, once the witness begins to push back.

Control your pace. Don't start talking too quickly, as if a rapid-fire pace will somehow trip up the witness. If you talk too fast, the jury will not understand your questions, which is the whole point of cross. Adopt the pace that will help the jury follow along. Speak in phrases, not whole sentences, as you deliver the key questions.

To clarify the meaning of each question, emphasize the key word or words in each one. A leading question is both a question to the witness and a presentation to the fact finder. Even when you are asking a short question, at least one word deserves emphasis.

You forgot to *send* the check, correct?

When you emphasize many words in a question, it sounds especially important.

You ... forgot ... to send ... the check, true?

Leading questions are, in reality, most often statements. It is possible to turn a statement into a question by using a rising questioning inflection at the end.

You never read that e-mail?

The rules allow this. Sometimes the statement is preceded by an interrogative phrase that turns it into a question.

Wouldn't you agree, you never read that e-mail?

Isn't it true that you never read that e-mail?

Isn't it correct, you never read that e-mail?

Am I right, you never read that e-mail?

You can also put the interrogative word at the end, but be careful not to repeat the same one over and over again.

You never read that e-mail, agreed?

You never read that e-mail, true?

You never read that e-mail, correct?

You never read that e-mail, right?

Leading questions should cover one fact at a time. Stringing several facts together can result in this problem:

Q: So you went out that night about 7:00 with a couple of friends and had several drinks, true?
A: No.

The cross examiner is now stuck. Which of those facts is incorrect? Is it the time she went out, the number of friends she went with, her personal definition of the word "several," or the quantity of drinks consumed? You can't know, so you can't fix the problem.

Practice out loud saying short questions containing only one fact per question. It is not the rhythm of conversational speech, so it requires mental discipline and practice.

Q: You went out that night, true?
A: Yes.
Q: At about 7:00?
A: Yes.
Q: You went with a couple of friends, right?
A: Yes.
Q: And you had three drinks?
A: Yes.

This is the only way to control your witness on cross.

Don't ignore the jury during cross. Since they are the most important people in the room, include them. Make eye contact with them occasionally. Use this technique on important questions you want the jury to think about.

Closing Argument

Closing argument is about connecting the dots, making inferences from the evidence, and drawing conclusions as to why your client should prevail. It is *not* time to retell the story. The jurors know what happened. They heard you preview the evidence during opening. The witnesses and exhibits fulfilled the promises you made then. Now, argue to them why you should win. Argue what that evidence means.

Argument requires energy. Advocacy is about the facts and the law, but human beings make decisions partly based on their feelings. To be persuasive, argue with an energy and sincerity that transmits to the jury your feeling about the facts and the rightness of your position.

A good theme for your opening statement will serve you well during closing argument. Repeat it. Now that all the evidence is in, the jury will understand it in a different way:

> I told you during opening statement that this would be a case about choices. Now you know that defendant is responsible for what happened because of her choices.

Your argument will review all those choices and argue why those choices mean that your client should prevail. A good theme is like the refrain of song that is repeated. Bring it back and "sing it again."

> Let's examine each of her choices.
> First, she chose ...
> Second, she chose ...

The theme helps you structure your argument. It is the lens through which the jury sees your whole case. You want the jury to silently sing along with your theme so that in jury deliberations they are singing your tune. They find themselves agreeing, "She did make that choice."

Alternatively, if your theme on opening was *Desperate men do desperate things*, your argument will review all the facts that proved he was desperate before reviewing all the evidence of his desperate actions.

> Now you know, members of the jury, that the defendant was truly desperate. Let's go over the evidence about his desperate finances.

Marshal those facts to make your point about his financial desperation.

Next, let's examine the evidence that proves his desperate act to burn down his company.

Teaching and arguing are closely related activities. Be a good teacher as you argue. Teach the jury to see the facts your way, and not from the perspective of opposing counsel. The best teacher wins. Adopt a pace that is appropriate to the complexity of the case and the composition of your jury. On your key points, stop and let the jury think about the point you have just made. Silence is persuasive. Don't rush on to make your next point. Let the argument sink in. You want to teach the jury your arguments so that some of them can repeat what you have said during their deliberations, to persuade their fellow jurors. You are teaching the jurors most inclined to your perspective to be your advocates during deliberations.

Use the language from the jury instruction and insert key phrases in your argument: "He failed to fulfill that duty …" "It was reasonable, foreseeable …" "She is entitled to recover …" Jurors don't use legal language in everyday conversation, but you prime them to do so by using key words and phrases in your argument.

Argument can be described as the time when you "add up." In a friendly conversational argument, someone who is not persuaded will say that it just doesn't add up. Drawing inferences and arriving at conclusions can be thought of as adding up the facts. Argument is like arithmetic: Fact A (specific testimony) + Fact B (a document) + Fact C (expert opinion) = Your conclusion. Add it up for the members of the jury: A + B + C = Conclusion. Note how this kind of structure is completely different from the arc of storytelling in opening statement. Argument is taking specific details from a variety of stories, as told by witnesses, and adding them together to reach your unassailable conclusion.

As you connect the dots and add it up, make sure you give your jury enough time to process the complexities of what is being said. They are not persuaded as you say it; they are persuaded once they have had a moment to think about what you said. Offer them time to think. Use this instruction at key moments in your argument: "He lost millions of dollars. His business was failing. He had a huge loan coming due. Yet he raised his fire insurance coverage ... right before the fire. Think about it, members of the jury." Pause. That is when the persuasion happens.

End strong. The only way to do that is to know exactly what you will say at the end and say it with confidence. Ask the jury to find in your favor. Practice saying the ending over and over again. Don't just think about it, but say it out loud. Don't trail off in volume, but be loud through to the final consonant of the final word.

Summary

Many attorneys have limited opportunities to get into court and try cases. To compensate for that reality, integrate these communication skills into your daily professional and personal conversations. Develop your skills as a questioner when talking with family, friends, and colleagues.

Mindfully ask open-ended questions when you make a new acquaintance, interview a potential client, or participate in a job interview. Be conscious of the fact that the form of your questions will either get someone else talking or elicit merely a *yes* or *no* response. Be aware of your own gestures in conversation and notice how other people talk and think with their hands.

Choose the appropriate attitude when discussing a difficult problem with your significant other. Hone your storytelling skills at a family gathering in anticipation of opening statement. Practice marshaling facts and arguing conclusions in a friendly conversational argument with a close friend.

All of these communication skills may be practiced and refined in daily conversation. The more you think about and use them, the better prepared you will be when the opportunity arises to take a case to trial. You will be ready to confidently respond when you hear that electrifying instruction, "Counsel, you may proceed."

Talk to Yourself

"Carefully select my attitude, tone, and demeanor."

"Gesture immediately; loosen up and open up."

"Start my opening statement with a theme and avoid starting with clichés."

"During direct, be curious and interested and the jury will, too."

"Use open-ended questions to help make the witness the star."

"Do not default to hostility and aggression during cross."

"Adopt a pace that will help the jury follow along."

"Persuasion happens when I pause."

"Practice my closing so I will end strong with confidence."

Appendices

Appendix One

Speaker's Checklist
Coordinating your body, your brain, and your voice for effective advocacy

Controlling Your Body

- Before it is your turn to speak, get conscious control of your breath by inhaling deeply and exhaling slowly.
- Continue to breathe deeply and slowly as you walk to the lectern.
- Relax your facial expression; release any tension from your mouth or eyebrows.
- Adopt a dynamic stance: center your weight evenly on both feet. Don't slouch or lean on lecterns or tables.
- Make eye contact with all your jurors before you start talking. Systematically look at those seated at the four corners of the jury perimeter.
- Look up from your notes and focus on the judge, jury, or witness before you speak. Before you ask your first question, make eye contact with the witness.
- Place your hands in the ready position, loosely touching at waist height with elbows bent at 90 degrees.
- Prepare to gesture before you speak, then instruct your body to release the gestures as you talk.
- Inhale consciously one last time before uttering your first sentence. This breath will support and project your voice. Breathe in, speak out.
- Remember the three Rs of natural gesturing: *ready* to gesture, *release* gestures, and *relax* your arms at your sides occasionally.
- Channel the adrenaline created by exhilaration and/or anxiety into big, smooth gestures.
- Gestures that are larger in size and longer in duration will make you feel and appear more natural.
- Get some "air in the armpits" and your gestures will look and feel more natural.
- Gesture from the shoulder, not just from the elbow.
- Plan and practice an initial trigger gesture to help jump-start your natural instinct to talk with your hands.
- Trigger gestures: *give* (facts or questions), *chop* (emphasis), or *show* (on the one

hand … on the other hand).

- Smoothly fill your natural zone of gesture, a rectangular space approximately four feet wide by two feet high.
- Gesture with open hands and open palms; don't curl your fingers inward.
- When asking questions, use the palms-up questioning gesture.
- Once you jump-start your initial gestures, stop thinking about them and let your instinct take over.

Controlling Your Brain

- Don't tell yourself to "Relax!" Instead, raise and release your energy as you begin speaking.
- To focus your brain, talk to people, not paper. Don't look at notes during your opening sentences or questions.
- Imagine you are speaking with individuals, not talking to an impersonal, monolithic jury.
- Don't be surprised at your listeners' stoic, deadpan facial expressions. (It has nothing to do with you!)
- Recognize the time warp created by adrenaline; plan to speak slowly at the start to compensate for your altered perception of time.
- Pauses are good; silence is golden. Short pauses give you time to think ahead and listeners time to absorb.
- Lay out the structure of your presentation for the jury. Saying it aloud will help you remember it, too.
- Reveal your enthusiasm and interest in your case, and be appropriately friendly.
- Realize that your jury can't tell how nervous you are inside; take comfort in that.
- Be patient and don't hit the panic button when you need to mentally search for your next word or idea.
- Use headlines to announce new topics during examinations: "Now let's focus on …"
- When using notes, less is more! Use bullet points. Resist reading from your notes.
- Don't be afraid to look at your notes between topics. Listeners only object when you talk to your notes.
- Notes are a visual aid for you, so write big and keep them simple. Put notes where they are easy to see.
- Try using horizontal notes, to match how you think and gesture.

- Less is more with PowerPoint and other forms of electronic images. Help your listeners absorb information on a screen by pausing, pointing, and giving them time to process what they see.

Controlling Your Voice

- Breathe deeply and vigorously. The power of your speaking voice is proportional to your breath support.
- To control the pace, speak in phrases, not whole sentences. Use the rhythm of the Pledge of Allegiance.
- Breathe consciously as a witness answers, in order to refill your lungs.
- Vary the pace: speak in phrases on important points, and speak more briskly for preliminary information.
- Control any unconscious thinking noises—such as *um* and *uh*—by consciously substituting silence instead.
- Emphasis creates meaning. Speak dynamically to stress the key words or phrases in every sentence or question.
- Recognize that words deserving emphasis are often at the ends of sentences or questions.
- Emphasize the endings of your sentences to keep your voice from trailing off.
- Beware the pitfall of repetitively ending sentences with a rising inflection, making it sound as if you are asking a question or making a list.
- To sound confident and conclusive, lower the pitch of your voice (not the volume) when ending sentences.
- Avoid excessive use of the conjunction *and* to connect your sentences and questions.
- Escape monotone delivery by putting emphatic stress on key words.
- Slow down and speak in more deliberate phrases when discussing complicated issues.

Practicing Aloud

- Practice on your feet to coordinate your body, brain, and voice.
- Practice aloud to build the muscle memory of your articulators: lips, tongue, jaw.
- Rough draft aloud; talk first, write second.

- Practice aloud while you are driving.
- Don't practice talking to a mirror. Mirrors merely make you more self-conscious.
- Practice aloud, alone, a lot!
- If you have limited time, always practice the first paragraph aloud several times so you can start strong.
- If you have limited time, always practice the last paragraph aloud several times so you can end strong.

Appendix Two

Video Self-Review Checklist
Critiquing yourself on video

Feet & Stance

- Is your stance dynamic? Are your feet a comfortable distance apart?
- Is your body weight centered so it is evenly balanced over both feet?
- Watch to see if you stand still at the beginning.
- Are your ankles crossed? Uncross them!
- Notice whether your feet are shuffling or shifting. Move only with a purpose, not randomly; occasionally walk to a new location when changing topics. Shifting only a couple of feet looks like nervous fidgeting. Move at least six feet when you decide to walk to a new location.
- Look at your feet. Are they moving more than your arms? Feet tend to move too much when the arms move too little. Think: Let your arms do the walking.

Knees & Hips

- Knees should be flexible, as they are when you are standing in a moving bus or subway. Don't lock them.
- Your hips should be centered over your feet. Avoid resting your weight on one hip, casually leaning to one side.

Breath Support

- Observe your breathing. Breathe consciously before you stand up; this helps control the adrenaline rush and calm your nerves.
- Can you see your lungs expanding and contracting? Breathe deeply from your abdominal area to project your voice and flood your brain with oxygen.

Gestures

- Are your hands in the ready position? Hands should be touching at your navel, elbows bent 90 degrees.

- Avoid the fig leaf position, the reverse fig leaf, hands in your pockets, or holding your pen.
- Gestures should be larger in size and longer in duration in order to look and feel natural.
- Natural gestures are smoother rather than jerkier, and slower rather than faster. Think smooth and slow.
- When do you begin to gesture? Consciously gesture sooner rather than later. Jump-start gestures immediately.
- Do you use the "on the one hand … on the other hand" gesture to trigger your instinct to gesture?
- You should fill the zone of gesture: a two-by-four-feet rectangle, two feet from your waist to your chin and four feet out to the sides.
- Are you gesturing when asking questions by extending the arms with palms up? *Give* the question with your gesture.
- Check to see if you use all four options to give questions: right hand, left hand, both hands, and, sometimes, none.
- Watch for *show* gestures. Could your hands be more expressive?
- Look for the karate *chop* or double karate chop with your hands sideways for the most emphatic delivery.
- If there is a lectern, are you touching it at all? Don't lean on the lectern with locked elbows, shoving your shoulders up toward your ears. Don't slouch on the lectern, placing your forearms on the furniture. Stand up straight.
- Observe whether you drop your arms to your sides—the *release* position—as you finish a thought. Be your own exclamation mark!

Posture

- Look at your body's alignment. Good posture is not shoulders back and chest out. That increases tension.
- Good posture is a direction—upward—not a position that is held like a statue.
- Your head belongs over your torso, not out front in a "chicken neck" position (don't lift your chin).
- Imagine your head is being pulled upward by a bungee cord attached to the top of your skull.

Face

- Is your face alive? Adopt your natural face of "introduction," the one you use when you shake hands while introducing yourself.
- Beware the deadpan "cadaver face." Try parting your lips slightly. Breathe through your mouth and nose.
- Notice whether your face and gestures are working together. Natural gestures tend to bring natural animation to your facial expressions.
- Don't freeze up! Keep gesturing.

Eyes

- Are you looking at your listeners? Did you focus on the fact finders or the witness before you began speaking?
- You should look at the four corners of the perimeter of your jury to define the target area.
- Understand your "thinking mannerism": When considering what to say next, do you look up, down, or sideways? Don't look away from people for too long.
- Focus your eyes to focus your brain.

Thinking

- Don't read to them! *Talk* to them. Which are you doing?
- Are there pauses in your delivery? Silence is golden. Silence is your friend.
- Adrenaline's time warp makes pauses seem inordinately long. Do they seem too long on video, or just about right?
- Have you given yourself and your listeners time to think?
- Time your pauses. How many seconds pass during each one? One second? Two?
- Where are you looking? Don't start by looking at and reading from your notes. Focus on the people you are addressing.
- You should use your notes like a parachute; go to them if you are about to crash and burn.
- Are your notes easy to read? Construct your notes as a visual aid for yourself: write big and keep it simple.

- Check to see whether you have defaulted to a furrowed brow.
- Actively choose your attitude. Attitude is a tactical choice.

Speaking

- You should hear yourself speak in phrases, not whole sentences. As you begin, use the pace of the Pledge of Allegiance.
- Listen to your pace. Do you start slowly by speaking in phrases, then speed up as you get comfortable?
- A slow pace signals the importance of what you are saying. Preliminary information may be faster. Persuasive points should be slower.
- Have you varied your pace? Separate … every … word occasionally to achieve a super-slow pace for extra emphasis. Use this technique when you quote documents, witnesses, evidence.
- Speaking too softly? Use more breath support.
- Is your voice trailing off? Emphasize the final word or phrase in questions.
- Listen for the questioning uptick of inflection at the ends of sentences. Do you sound uncertain?
- Do you drop the pitch of your voice to end sentences conclusively?
- Listen to hear whether you walk down the steps. Think of how newscasters sign off at the end of a broadcast.

The Law of Opposites

- Have you applied the Law of Opposites? For a sentence or even just a phrase, have you done the opposite of what your instinct most often leads you to do?
- Listen carefully to hear whether you go slower than your usual pace for emphasis, or speak softer than your usual volume for emphasis.
- Make sure you are still on occasion, not just animated.
- Listen for contrast. Do you ever use longer silences to let the fact finder think?
- Notice whether the "s" words could apply to your performance: slower, softer, still, and silence.

Appendix Three

Essential Delivery Skills While Sitting for Arbitration

- Get control of your breathing—deep and slow—while waiting for your turn to speak.
- Sit up straight with both feet on the floor. Don't slouch in your chair.
- Place legible, easy-to-read notes before you. Use horizontal notes. (refer to page 80)
- Push your notes forward slightly so they are easy to read as you speak.
- Separate your hands resting on the table, allowing you to gesture naturally.
- Don't fidget nervously with your pen, notes, paperclips, etc. Keep hands free.
- Take a deep breath in the silence as you consult your notes before speaking.
- Make eye contact as you breathe in once more, and then speak out with that breath.
- Gesture immediately as you begin to speak. Loosen up as quickly as possible.
- To control your pace, speak in phrases—not whole sentences—as you talk.
- *Do not read a script.* Talk to and look at the arbitrator or witness, not your notes.

Appendix Four

Essential Delivery Skills to Argue a Motion or Appeal

- Get control of your breathing—deep and slow—while waiting your turn to speak.
- Once at the lectern, adopt a centered stance with your weight balanced on both feet.
- Place your legible, easy-to-read, horizontal notes on the lectern. (refer to page 80)
- Take a step back allowing you to see your notes easily without bobbing your head.
- Bring your hands up to the ready position, loosely touching at waist height.
- Take a deep breath in silence as you consult your notes before speaking.
- Make eye contact with the bench, breathe in one final time, and then speak out.
- Gesture immediately as you begin to speak. Loosen up as quickly as possible.
- Speak in phrases—not whole sentences—as you tell the court the remedy you seek.
- *Do not read.* Talk to and look at the judge or judges you are addressing.
- Make your strongest argument first, or address immediately a critical issue just heard from opposing counsel.
- Maintain eye contact as you scan the bench for signals that a question is coming.
- Be assertive and respectful. Stop talking immediately when a judge speaks.
- Never interrupt a judge who is asking you a question.
- Avoid "With all due respect, Your Honor," which many judges find disrespectful and condescending.
- When you disagree say, "We disagree, Your Honor. Our argument is…"
- It is best to begin your answer with a "Yes" or "No," before explaining.
- Collect and use phrases that pivot back to your argument: "Your Honor, that brings me back to our reason for asking to deny their motion." Or "That supports our argument for granting our motion."

- Be prepared to recap your main points and conclude briefly in about 30 seconds.
- In advance of your argument, *practice out loud* requests for concessions, relevant case law, and answering opposing arguments.
- Anticipate possible hypotheticals.
- Practice arguing aloud issues of public policy, law, and justice related to the issues.

Bibliography

Alibali, Martha W., Miriam Bassok, Karen Olseth Solomon, Sharon E. Syc, and Susan Goldin-Meadow. "Illuminating Mental Representations through Speech and Gesture." *Psychological Science* 10, no. 4 (July 1999): 327–33.

Amberry, Tom, and Philip Reed. *Free Throw: 7 Steps to Success at the Free Throw Line.* New York: HarperCollins, 1996.

Burns, Ken. *The Civil War,* film. Washington, DC: Public Broadcasting Service, 1990.

Garner, Bryan A. "What Judges Really Think About the Phrase 'May It Please the Court.'" *Bryan Garner on Words* (blog), ABA *Journal* (April 1, 2013). http://www.abajournal.com/magazine/article/what_judges_really_think_about_the_phrase_may_it_please_the_court.

Gawande, Atul. *Complications: A Surgeon's Notes on an Imperfect Science.* New York: Picador, 2002.

Goldin-Meadow, Susan. *Hearing Gesture: How Our Hands Help Us Think.* Cambridge, MA: Belknap Press, 2003.

Holzer, Harold. *Lincoln at Cooper Union: The Speech That Made Abraham Lincoln President.* New York: Simon & Schuster, 2004.

Iverson, Jana M. "Gesture When There Is No Visual Model." In *The Nature and Functions of Gesture in Children's Communication: New Directions for Child Development, No. 79*, edited by Jana M. Iverson and Susan Goldin-Meadow, 89–100. San Francisco: Jossey-Bass, Spring 1998.

Kendon, Adam. "An Agenda for Gesture Studies." *Semiotic Review of Books* 7, no. 3 (1996): 8–12. http://projects.chass.utoronto.ca/semiotics/srb/gesture.html.

Kendon, Adam, ed. "Gesture and Understanding in Social Interaction." Special issue, *Research on Language and Social Interaction 27*, no. 3 (1994).

McNeill, David. *Hand and Mind: What Gestures Reveal about Thought.* Chicago: University of Chicago Press, 1992.

Ornstein, Robert E. *On the Experience of Time.* Boulder, CO: Westview Press, 1997.

Rothschild, Frank D., and Deanne C. Siemer. *Basic PowerPoint Exhibits.* Boulder, CO: National Institute for Trial Advocacy, 2003.

Stattkus, Dietmar. *Help! I'm Sweating! Causes, Phenomena, Therapies.* Wuppertal, Germany: Hidrex, Biomedizinische Technik, 2006.

Tufte, Edward R. *The Cognitive Style of PowerPoint: Pitching Out Currupts Within.* 2nd ed. Chesire, CT: Graphics Press, 2006.

Williams, Ted, and John Underwood. *The Science of Hitting.* New York: Simon & Schuster, 1986.

Wilson, Frank R. *The Hand: How Its Use Shapes the Brain, Language, and Human Culture.* New York: Pantheon Books, 1998.

Index

A

acting and speaking (similarities)
  emphasis and meaning, 127–129
  and practicing speaking, 154
adrenaline
  and conscious body control, 12–14
  effects on body, 12
  eye contact and blushing, 61–62
  and paradox of naturalness, 8
  and perception of time, 66–69, 117–118
  and rapid speech, 66
  and rate of breathing, 23
  and standing still, 18
advocacy
  authentic persuasive style, 7, 10
  credibility and conscious body control, 12
alignment. *See* posture and alignment
Amberry, Tom, 14–15
ankles, 17
anxiety
  and adrenaline, 13
  overcoming, 178
appeals delivery skills checklist, 216–217
arbitration delivery skills checklist, 215
arms
  ready, release, and relax gestures, 41–42
  zone of gesture, 35, 51
art of natural gestures, 31–32
articulation, 112
athletes
  and adrenaline, 13
  and structured improvisation, 76
  and zone of concentration, 69
attention span. *See* listening
attitude
  and cross examinations, 95
  practicing, 173
  as a tactical choice, 93–96
  tone of voice and attitude, 146
audible punctuation and intonation, 142–144
authentic persuasive style
  described, 7
  mastery of technique for, 10
  See also personal style
authoritative audibility, 9
autonomic nervous system, 24

B

back, lower back muscle relaxation, 20
"baton gestures," 50
blindness and gesturing, 29–30
blushing, 61–62
body
  confidence and conscious body control, 12, 63–64
  lower body control, 16–22
  mannerisms and paradox of naturalness, 8
  physical checklists, 14–16, 64, 157, 207–208
  standing still, 18, 167
  See also face; posture and alignment
brain
  adrenaline and the time warp, 66–69
  checklists, 104, 208–209
  chunking of information, 90
  and echo memory, 71–73
  gesturing and horizontal notes format, 80–84
  knowing vs. knowing how, 151–152
  mirror neurons, 96–97
  oxygenation of, 27
  and paradox of naturalness, 9
  prefrontal cortex and physical rituals, 15

purposeful movement, 21
reading and talking simultaneously, 77
science of natural gestures, 29–31
and structured improvisation, 75–76
and zone of concentration, 69–71
"breath support," 26–27
breathing
   and brain oxygenation, 27
   breathing in and speaking out, 26–27
   conscious breathing effects, 23–24
   conscious breathing mechanics, 24–26, 107–109
   practicing, 178–179
   video self-review checklist, 211
   and vocal fatigue, 110–111
brow, furrowed brow, 58
Bryan, William Jennings, 109
Burns, Ken, 127

C

centering your hips, 19–20
checklists
   arbitration delivery skills, 215
   brain, 104, 208–209
   motions and appeals, 216–217
   physical checklists, 14–16, 64, 157, 207–208
   practicing, 180
   trial skills, 203
   video self-review, 211–214
   voice, 148, 209
chop gesture, 42–43, 44–45, 47, 48–49
chunking of information, 90, 103, 117–118
closing arguments
   and attitude/demeanor, 95
   practicing, 139–140
   skills development, 199–202
Complications (Gawande), 61
confidence
   and conscious body control, 12
   ending with confidence, 144–145

conscious body control, 12
conscious breathing
   effects, 23–24
   mechanics, 24–25, 107–109
conscious muscle control, 20
courtroom movement, 20
credibility
   attitude as tactical choice, 93–96
   confidence and conscious body control, 12
Croft, Peter, 69
cross examinations
   and attitude/demeanor, 95
   elimination of saying "and," 172
   skills development, 197–199
crossed ankles, 17

D

Death of a Salesman (play), 128
demeanor
   and cross examinations, 95
   practicing, 173
diaphragm. *See* lungs and diaphragm
direct examinations
   and attitude/demeanor, 94
   and deep breathing, 109
   effortless nature of, 9
   elimination of saying "okay," 170–172
   practicing, 139
   and reading from notes, 73–74
   skills development, 190–197
   structured improvisation, 75–76
duration
   and emphasis, 130–131
   of gestures, 35

E

echo memory, 71–73
electronic evidence presentation, 97–102
   explaining slide content, 100
   identifying screen content for the re-

cord, 98–99
importance of, 97
outlines for opening or closing, 101
practicing, 163–164
reading and absorbing text, 100–101
reading and listening simultaneously, 98
telling jurors what they are looking at, 99–100
timing of slides, 102
turning slides off periodically, 102
emotions
and jury selection, 184
and mirror neurons, 96–97
and practicing speaking, 154–155
emphasis
chop gesture, 42–43, 44–45
and gestures, 134–141
and meaning, 123–129
volume, pitch, and duration, 129–131
energy and persuasive speech, 116–117
excitement balanced with nervousness, 14
eye contact
and blushing, 61–62
controlled focus, 62
duration of, 62
importance of, 58–59
and pacing, 63
practicing, 168–169
and referring to notes, 63
sustained eye contact, 21–22
video self-review checklist, 213
when speaking under pressure, 59–62

F
face
about, 56
eye contact, 58–63
furrowed brow, 58
mouth and lips, 56–57
video self-review checklist, 213
and warming up your voice, 113–114
fatigue and centering your hips, 19–20

Federer, Roger, 69
feet
planting your feet, 16–18
standing still, 18, 167
video self-review checklist, 211
fig leaf position, 37, 39
fight-or-flight response, 13, 62
finger wagging, 50
flexible knees, 18–19
Free Throw (Amberry), 14–15
furrowed brow, 58

G
Garner, Bryan, 122
Gawande, Atul, 61
gesturing
about, 28–29, 51
art of natural gestures, 31–32
distracting gestures, 50
and emphasis, 134–135
give, chop, and show, 42–47, 48–49
and holding a pen, 51
and horizontal notes format, 80–85
impulse to gesture, 35–36
jump-starting and practicing, 32–33
and monotone, 135–136
pacing and conducting yourself, 136
practicing, 32–33, 137–140, 158–159, 161
and the ready position, 37–41
ready, release, and relax, 41–42
science of natural gestures, 29–31
"on the shelf" gestures, 47–49, 81–82
smoothness of, 136–137
video self-review checklist, 211–212
zone of gesture, 33–35, 51
Gettysburg Address, 109, 127, 129
give gesture, 42–44, 47, 48–49
Goldin-Meadow, Susan, 31, 34

H

Hamlet's Advice to the Players, 31
Hand and Mind (McNeill), 31
The Hand (Wilson), 31
hands. *See* gesturing; the ready position
head alignment, 52–53
Hearing Gesture (Goldin-Meadow), 31, 34
heart rate, adrenaline and perception of time, 68–69
high heels, 20
hips
    centering your hips, 19–20
    video self-review checklist, 211
holding a pen and gesturing, 51
hyperventilation, 23

I

improvisation, structured, 75–76
impulse to gesture, 35–36
intonation, 142–144
invisible ready position, 39
Iverson, Jana, 29–30, 31, 134

J

jury selection, 182–186

K

Kendon, Adam, 31
Kennedy, John F., 120, 131
knees
    flexible knees, 18–19
    video self-review checklist, 211
knowing vs. knowing how, 151–152

L

larynx and vocal cords, 111–112
law of opposites and personal style, 176–177, 214
leading questions and jury selection, 186
Lincoln, Abraham, 109, 127

lips and mouth, 56–57
listening
    echo memory, 71–73
    focus on eyes of speaker, 39
    gestures and memory, 30–31
    listener's perspective and horizontal notes format, 84–85
    primacy and recency, 90–93
    and purposeful movement, 20–22
    silence and zone of concentration, 69–71
    to yourself, 106–107
loose gestures, 36
lower back muscle relaxation, 20
lower body control, 16–22
    centering your hips, 19–20
    flexible knees, 18–19
    planting your feet, 16–18
    and purposeful movement, 20–22
    standing still, 18
lungs and diaphragm
    conscious breathing mechanics, 24–25, 107–109
    intercostal muscles and rib cage, 108
    larynx and vocal cords, 111–112
    projecting your voice with breath, 109–110
    respiration and "butterflies in your stomach," 13
    and vocal fatigue, 110–111

M

mannerisms
    adrenaline and conscious body control, 14
    and paradox of naturalness, 8
mechanics
    of phrasing and pace, 118–120
    of readiness, 40
memory
    chunking of information, 90
    echo memory, 71–73

and gestures, 30–31
planning to forget, 86–88
and structured improvisation, 75–76
"minding the gap" and elimination of thinking noises, 124–125, 169–170
mirror neurons, 96–97
monotone, 135–136
motions delivery skills checklist, 216–217
mouth and lips, 56–57
movement
    fatigue and centering your hips, 19–20
    purposeful, 20–22
    random movement and standing still, 18
muscles
    conscious control of, 20
    lower back muscle relaxation, 20
    respiration and "butterflies in your stomach," 13

N
naturalness
    authentic persuasive style, 7
    paradox of, 7–10
neck alignment, 52–53
nervousness
    and adrenaline, 13–14
    and conscious breathing, 23–24, 26
    energy and persuasive speech, 116–117
    impulse to gesture, 35–36
"neutral alert" appearance, 56–57
notes
    accessibility, 79–80
    and eye contact, 63
    horizontal notes format, 80–85
    large font size, 78
    legibility, 78–79
    and planning to forget, 86–88
    practicing with, 86, 163
    reading aloud, 133–134, 162
    reading and talking simultaneously, 77
    reading from notes, 73–74, 77

simplicity of, 79
video self-review checklist, 213–214
as visual aid, 77–78

O
On the Perception of Time (Ornstein), 67
"on the shelf" gestures, 47–49, 81–82
open-ended questions and jury selection, 185
opening statements
    and attitude/demeanor, 94
    practicing, 137–139, 159
    skills development, 186–190
openness and jury selection, 182–183
opera singers' volume and breath control, 110
Ornstein, Robert E., 67–68
oxygen, brain oxygenation, 27

P
pace of speech. See phrasing and pace
pacing
    and eye contact, 63
    and purposeful movement, 21–22
panic and adrenaline, 13
parade rest position, 37
performance pressures and release of adrenaline, 13
personal style
    authentic persuasive style, 7, 10
    and law of opposites, 176–177, 214
    and listening to yourself, 106–107
    lower body control, 16–22
    performance ritual, 14–16, 64
    personal anecdotes and structured improvisation, 75–76
    phrasing and pace, 115–122
    primacy and recency, 90–93
    and purposeful movement, 22
    role models for, 175
    tactical breathing, 23–27

See also gesturing; rituals; speaking
phrasing and pace
    conducting yourself, 136
    deliberate sentence beginnings, 122
    emphasis and meaning, 123–129
    mechanics of, 118–120
    and persuasive speech, 116–118
    practicing, 167–168
    setting the pace, 121–122
    varying the pace, 120–121
pitch
    and emphasis, 129–130
    and intonation, 142–144
planting your feet, 16–18
pockets and gesturing, 36, 39
pointing gestures, 50
posture and alignment
    good posture, 52
    neck and head, 52–53
    sitting, 54–55
    spine, 53–54
    video self-review checklist, 212
practicing
    attitude and demeanor, 173
    avoidance of, 154–155
    beginning of leading questions, 172
    beginning of presentations, 159
    breathing, 178–179
    checklists, 180
    courtroom rituals, 164–165
    elimination of saying "okay," 170–172
    elimination of thinking noises, 169–170
    ending of presentations, 160
    gesturing, 32–33, 137–140, 158–159, 161
    importance of, 150–151, 153, 179
    informal sessions, 173–177
    knowing vs. knowing how, 151–152
    mental preparation, 177–179
    notes and visual aids, 163–164
    patience necessary for, 155
    phrasing and pace, 167–168
    reading aloud, 162
    recitation, 162
    speaking aloud, 174, 209–210
    speaking in phrases, 158
    standing still, 167
    talking first and writing second, 159
    transitions and headlines, 160–161
    using a mirror, 153
    using video, 165–166, 178
    verbal skills, 146–148
    volume, 166–167
    warming up your voice, 157–158
primacy and recency, 90–93
projecting your voice with breath, 109–110
prosody and natural conversation, 141–145
psyching yourself up, 177–178
purposeful movement, 20–22

R

random movement and standing still, 18
reading from notes. See notes
the ready position
    described, 37–38
    and holding a pen, 51
    invisible ready position, 39
    mechanics of readiness, 40
    secret handshake position, 40–41
    and using alternative positions, 39
ready, release, and relax, 41–42
recency and primacy, 90–93
recitation, 74–75, 89
repetitive gestures, 50
respiration, nervousness and "butterflies in your stomach," 13
reverse fig leaf position, 37, 39
rituals
    physical checklists, 14–16, 64, 157, 207–208
    psyching yourself up, 177–178
Rodenburg, Patsy, 27
Rothschild, Frank R., 102

S

saying "okay," 170–172
science of natural gestures, 29–31
scripting, 89
secret handshake position, 40–41
self-consciousness and paradox of naturalness, 7–8
setting your speaking pace, 121–122
Shakespeare on natural gestures, 31
shoes, high heels, 20
shoulders
   and good posture, 52
   neck and head alignment, 53
   spine alignment, 53–54
show gesture, 42–43, 45–47, 48–49
silence
   and conscious body control, 14
   and deliberate sentence beginnings, 122
   and echo memory, 72–73
   elimination of thinking noises, 124–125
   and persuasive speech, 115–116
   phrasing and pace, 167–168
   and planning to forget, 87–88
   and zone of concentration, 69–71
sitting posture and alignment, 54–55
smooth gestures, 36
speaking
   about, 103
   adrenaline and rapid speech, 66
   appeals delivery skills, 216–217
   arbitration delivery skills, 215
   attitude as tactical choice, 93–96
   breathing in and speaking out, 26–27
   chunking of information, 90
   courtroom delivery skills, 14–16, 64, 157, 207–208
   electronic evidence presentation, 97–102
   elimination of thinking noises, 123–125, 169–170
   emphasis and meaning, 123–131
   ending with confidence, 144–145
   motions delivery skills, 216–217
   persuasive phrasing and pacing, 115–122
   phrasing and pace, 115–122, 158, 167–168
   pitfalls of reading, 131–133
   planning to forget, 86–88
   practicing aloud, 174, 209–210
   practicing verbal skills, 146–148
   primacy and recency, 90–93
   prosody and natural conversation, 141–145
   reading and talking simultaneously, 77
   recitation, 74–75, 89
   scripting, 89
   silence and zone of concentration, 69–71
   structured improvisation, 75–76
   talking first and writing second, 159
   thinking backward, 89
   thinking noises, 9, 69–70, 123–125
   trial delivery skills, 203
   video self-review checklist, 214
   and visualization, 140–141
   volume, 166–167
   when reading is required, 133–134
   See also eye contact; gesturing; notes; practicing; voice
spine alignment, 53–54
sports psychology and ritualized actions, 15
stage performers' volume and breath control, 110
stance
   flexible knees, 18–19
   planting your feet, 16–18
   standing still, 18, 167
   video self-review checklist, 211
stillness and purposeful movement, 21–22
structured improvisation, 75–76
style. *See* personal style
"subway knees," 18–19
sustained eye contact, 21–22

T

tactical breathing, 23–27
technique and authentic persuasive style, 10
thinking noises
    elimination of, 123–125, 169–170
    and speaking with finesse, 9
    and zone of concentration, 69–70
thinking on your feet. *See* notes; speaking
the Three Rs of natural gestures
    give, chop, and show, 42–47
    ready, release, and relax, 41–42
    "on the shelf" gestures, 47–49, 81–82
thumb puppet gesture, 50
time, perception of, 66–69
tone of voice and attitude, 146
torso. *See* posture and alignment
touch, turn, talk (visual aids), 163
trial skills
    checklist, 203
    closing arguments, 199–202
    cross examinations, 197–199
    delivery skills for arguing a motion or an appeal, 216–217
    development of, 152, 155, 202–203
    direct examinations, 190–197
    jury selection, 182–186
    opening statements, 186–190
Tufte, Edward R., 102

U

unamplified public speaking, 109
unnatural behaviors and paradox of naturalness, 7–10

V

varying your speaking pace, 120–121
video and practicing, 165–166, 178
viewing is doing, 96–97
visual communication and electronic evidence, 102

voice
    about, 106, 147–148
    articulation, 112
    authoritative audibility and paradox of naturalness, 9
    checklists, 148, 209
    intonation, 142–144
    larynx and vocal cords, 111–112
    listening to yourself, 106–107
    lungs and diaphragm, 107–115
    monotone, 135–136
    projecting your voice with breath, 109–110
    tone of voice and attitude, 146
    vocal fatigue, 110–111
    warming up, 113–115, 157–158
volume
    and emphasis, 129
    practicing, 166–167

W

warming up your voice, 113–115, 157–158
Williams, Ted, 69

Z

zone of concentration, 69–71
zone of gesture, 33–35, 51

About the Authors

BRIAN K. JOHNSON coaches hundreds of lawyers annually on improving their communication and persuasion skills. Able to offer individualized, immediately useful suggestions for improvement, he helps speakers gesture naturally and think clearly in high-stakes situations. He often coaches senior partners at firms where the best strive to be better.

Johnson has worked as a communication consultant to the legal profession for over thirty-five years. His communication lecture has been the opening event at the National Institute for Trial Advocacy's two-week national trial skills program since 1988. In 2000, he was presented with NITA's Honorable Prentice Marshall Faculty Award—the first nonlawyer in NITA's history to receive this honor.

In Estonia, Johnson has been part of a team training lawyers for that country's transition from an inquisitorial to an adversarial system. For the US Department of Justice, he lectures and coaches monthly for Assistant US Attorneys at the National Advocacy Center in Columbia, South Carolina. He also teaches annually at the Hillman Advocacy Program in Grand Rapids, Michigan. He has been a visiting lecturer in trial advocacy at the University of Tennessee, Temple School of Law, McGeorge School of Law, and the Queen's University Institute for Legal Studies in Belfast.

As a trial consultant, Johnson works with trial lawyers preparing witnesses to testify. He has consulted on cases involving Internet browsers, breast implants, medical devices, financial services, and the airline industry, as well as patent infringement cases that have won verdicts in the billions of dollars.

MARSHA HUNTER, a specialist in legal communication, trains attorneys to speak confidently and persuasively in all settings. Under her guidance, trial lawyers sharpen their advocacy skills and transactional attorneys refine their presentations, becoming more articulate, fluent, and eloquent. Hunter teaches lawyers, and only lawyers, in the arts of oral advocacy and public and professional speaking.

As a principal in Johnson and Hunter, Inc., Hunter has legal clients in the United States, Canada, Australia, and Europe. She teaches communication skills for the National Institute for Trial Advocacy, the US Department of Justice, the American Bar Association, elite law firms and law schools, and bar associations and law societies from Belfast to Tasmania.

Hunter has published articles in numerous legal publications, including the American Bar Association Section of Litigation's *The Woman Advocate*, the *Texas Bar Journal, PD Quarterly, NALP Bulletin, The Legal Advocate*, and others. She posts on *The Articulate Attorney* blog on topics ranging from how celebrities gesture to the art of speaking within your own natural vocal pitch and inflection.

Also by Brian K. Johnson and Marsha Hunter

The Articulate Attorney:
Public Speaking for Lawyers
Crown King Books, 2013

The Articulate Witness:
An Illustrated Guide to Testifying Confidently Under Oath
Crown King Books, 2015